The Intoxicating Hotwife

The

Intoxicating

Hotwife

Scarlett Carrington

TENTH STREET PRESS

THIS EDITION

ISBN-10: 0-6481676-3-1
ISBN-13: 978-0-6481676-3-1

TENTH STREET PRESS Ltd.
MELBOURNE LONDON
www.tenthstreetpress.com
Email: contact@tenthstreetpress.com

CONTENTS

INTRODUCTION

Scarlett Carrington is a modern, successful businesswoman in her early 30s. She has the perfect life: wonderful husband, beautiful home and intelligent sporty children. She works very hard to uphold her perfect image and reputation. This young professional is an upcoming executive type that doesn't take no for an answer. Scarlett and her husband Seth are very active volunteers in multiple communities through various organizations. Their extended families are in the public eye. Each person in each family plays their part to perfection, the part expected of their family lineage. She has a naughty secret – she loves to have sex! Scarlett is a Christian living in the Southeast; more accurately labeled the "Bible belt of the United States." In a society where one cuss word or one drink of alcohol can condemn you to hell, it would appear to be impossible for Mrs. Scarlett Carrington to enjoy a swinger lifestyle. She struggled with the idea of doing something that may seem immoral. She partakes in activities that she swore she would never allow herself to get tangled up in. At first, Scarlett and Seth participated in the swinger lifestyle together. In this novel you will see a young woman turn from an innocent Christian to a slutty HotWife while still holding tight to her faith and her perfect reputation. As long as there are no strings attached, it's not frequent, and Seth knows, it can't be considered cheating, right?

Carrington lived a perfect everyday life during the day and a hedonistic life by night. She would meet men of all walks of life, women that enjoy exploring another woman's body, and the occasional couple. Her mix of intellect, beauty, sexual aura, wit, creativity, and pure hedonistic kinkiness intoxicates every man she encounters. They become addicted and needy, causing her to cut all contact with them completely. Then, she met her weakness - Samson. She was blindsided by Samson. He had certain physical characteristics that she never liked in a man before she met him. He was married and that was Scarlett's cardinal sin for play. She would never play with a married man. Although she fought meeting him for a long time, something kept drawing her to him. He was everything she wanted and her body knew it the first time she met him. This man is different and she knew he would be something different for her. Follow the journey of The Intoxicating HotWife through her sexual escapades, entrance into the BDSM lifestyle, and conversion to finding her contentment in life. Explore fantasies through the eyes of Mrs. Carrington and watch this logical businesswoman fall for her lover. Scarlett's life is filled with lust, love, success, passion, excitement, and now contentment after achieving the lifestyle she had only dreamed of a decade earlier.

Our society has been inundated with sexy movies and novels. Women fantasize about how they want to have a man just like the one in the book. Women want to dress sexy and have a man lust after them. Women want passion, lust, and desire.

Many women think this is only a fantasy, only something they read in a book or see in a movie. They resign themselves to believing they cannot do such things based on their religious beliefs, because they are married, or because they're worried that someone may find out. So, they don't try. It's not that they don't want to. From the women I've spoken to, it's almost as if they believe they need permission to feel the way they do and want the things they want! Who says you need permission? Who says that you can't have everything you want in life as long as you're willing to do what it takes to get it? In a real life story of success, lust, love, and perfection, Scarlett explains how you can have it all in life while indulging in your every desire!

CHAPTER 1

I message Samson to let him know I'm going to a movie with my girlfriend. It was one of those sexy male stripper types of movies. You all know the popular series! He said, "girlfriend, huh?" I reply, "yes, girlfriend. I caught your suggestive tone! Don't worry baby, she and I already played once!" Samson tells me it's hot that I'm going to a movie about a bunch of male strippers with my bi girlfriend. I receive a few more messages asking what she and I have done in the past, what I'm wearing to the movie, etc. I walk through the doors of the movie theater and meet my girlfriend. I'm completely discreet about everything, so I want to have a fun girl's night out. We go in, find our seats, and tell each other how hot we both look! We get turned on by each other and by the movie. After the movie, we both planned to go home to our husbands. I message my lover Samson and he asks if I enjoyed the movie. I tell him how excited it made me and how wet I am! I get a message from my girlfriend and she's pissed because I wasn't all touchy feely with her in the theater. I can't be like that! I remind her again that I can't be open in public, but she's still mad. She and I have been through this before after a public event we attended. It was a large concert in which I could not touch her or say anything suggestive at all. After that concert, she and I went to walk by the river and found a nice landing where we could sit and make out while the sun was setting on the water. She is so much fun when we play! She's completely into licking me and wants to enjoy every inch of me as long as she can. But, she doesn't understand that I must be discreet because I can't ruin my perfect image.

So, I end the conversation and move back to my conversation with Samson. I don't do drama.

I tell him all the sexy things I just watched and how I would enjoy playing with the lead character. Samson is turned on and super flirty. He tells me he wants to see me, so I meet him at a local sports park. It's very close to a main road, but still very private. He arrives before I do and is standing outside of his vehicle. I get out of my SUV and walk over to him. We chit chat and flirt a bit. It isn't long until he's running his fingers inside the waist of my pants. Mmmm! He's such a tease! His touch is electric and I can't wait to find out how it feels to have him on top of me. I tell Samson I don't do stuff like this out in public and suggest we get into his big vehicle. We're passionately making out in the back of his large vehicle and I quickly pull my pants off. The windows are down and the weather is that hot, humid, sultry heat every Southerner knows to be commonplace of lustful summer evenings. Something takes over us during those types of evenings. We change into erotic creatures that seek out ways to fulfill our secret desires. The air is thick with desire. His seats are leather, so clean up should be easy. I make sure he has a condom because I need this man! I've been primed for hours and I want to be fucked! I slowly start unzipping his pants before I pull out his cock and smile. I think I knew right then and there that I would become addicted to Samson's cock. I loved how it felt in my mouth. He strokes my hair and moans every time I slid it all the way down my throat. I thought he was going to explode in my throat! He stops me by carefully pulling my head up. He kisses me long and hard. You know the kind of kiss I'm talking about. The kind of kiss that makes you forget where you are as long as you're with him! He has me lying back on the seat with my legs up in the air on the back of the seats. He opens them wide and starts licking me. Mmmmm… he's so good at that! I remember looking up and seeing the beautiful stars in the night sky above me thinking this couldn't be more perfect, intoxicating, and intense. Every little touch felt like my skin was on fire! I was so lost in the lust and desire of having him that I couldn't do anything except enjoy the moment! He starts fingering me and I'm about to cum. He pushes his pinky finger in my asshole and licks my clit even faster. Oh my God! I cum hard against his face, soaking his fingers! He fingers me hard all the way through my wave of orgasm. Samson pulls his fingers out and he licks my slit to clean up all the juices. This man, I swear! I suck him again for a few minutes and then he leans over me to kiss me. He pushes me back down while kissing me. I watch him roll the condom on his cock and watch him enter my pussy. It's so needy and greedy. I've wanted this from the moment I saw this man and now it's about to happen! He slowly enters me and lets me adjust to his size. I push my legs open farther so he can go in deeper. I feel his cock hit balls deep into me and I can't wait for him to start stroking his length in and out of me. My new lover and I fuck the sultry summer evening away until we both cum together in an intense orgasm. I am on cloud nine when we have to go. I kiss him goodbye and pray to God that's not the last time I see him!

I go home to my husband and give him a big hug. Have you ever seen the movie Stepford Wives? The families that live in Stepford appear to be perfect. We are part of families similar to the families in the movie. If you're on the outside looking in, we appear to be the perfect family. We both have good jobs. We are respectable, active members of multiple communities. We are active in multiple sports across multiple cities and states. We go to church. We dress well and are very well known where we live. Our families are employed within the fields of technology, law, law enforcement, education, religion, construction, banking, and healthcare just to name a few.

The first time I ever laid eyes on Samson who is now my Dom, sub, and lover was at a local dam. He was tall, well dressed and kind. I was concerned because I've never liked tall men nor men with facial hair and he had both! We chatted for a bit and then we kissed. I picked up on my attraction to him as soon as I saw him. The conversation went well. But, that kiss! I was blown away. It started out slow, sensual. The first kiss my lover and I shared grew passionate where he found the spot on the back of my neck that drives me wild and he pulled my hair a little. I remember moaning into Samson's mouth when he pulled my hair. We chatted a bit more before he held my hand and walked me back to our vehicles. I had been sick that day, but wanted to meet him. He was so kind, yet so passionate. So warm, yet he was so dominant and possessive. I wanted him. I swear I think I fell for this man the very first time I met him. I didn't know he would end up being such a vital part of my life. This was just supposed to be an easy, one time, NSA play arrangement. But, that day, I recognized I had met "Mine." Even when I had not been previously part of the BDSM lifestyle, I could feel in that moment that I had just met someone that meant something.

I message my husband and give him all the details of the first meeting. I meet him at home and for a family dinner.

CHAPTER 2

I'm a Christian. I've believed in God since I was a little girl. It was never a situation of believing because someone told me to or because I thought I should. I personally believe that Jesus died for my sins, and yours, to the core of my being. I live my life trying to be an example of how to live a good, Christ-centered life. I generally want to be a good person. I have multiple family members that went to seminary. I have relatives that hold positions within the church, including a preacher. I grew up in a family that debated education, religion, and politics. My husband and I were innocent virgins when we met and it was an amazing experience to save ourselves for each other.

I'm competitive, extroverted, and I overanalyze everything. I'm a terrific wife, mother, aunt, daughter, and granddaughter. I'm successful and happy, and learning to be content! That probably sounds cocky, but it's not. I'm confident.

I'm beautiful and intelligent. I also have a seductive, sultry, sinful side that's oh so yummy! I'm a swinger, and I'm active in a BDSM lifestyle. I love my husband dearly and he is literally my other half. He's everything I'm not. He completes me and challenges me. My husband and I have learned so much about life, the world, and each other by being together. I have children that are amazing. I couldn't be any more proud of them. They make great grades in school, are great athletes, have unique personalities, and already understand how to weigh options in all decisions to come to the best conclusion. In addition to that, I have a gentleman that serves as my Daddy Dom, sub, and lover all in one person! I couldn't have been any more fortunate to find someone so special!

You may be asking yourself how someone in a perfect, religious, family that's always in the public eye pulls all of this off. How does a woman give herself permission to enjoy the primal, carnal, seductive things she dreams about while still having the perfect life? It's actually very simple. I give myself permission. My husband gives me permission. We have a high level of trust for each other. My husband and I have basic rules for playing. We always have open, honest communication. You know you get turned on reading the popular sexy books and watching the movies. You may catch yourself getting turned on imagining what it would be like to have a sexy man open the door for you and spank your ass as you walk through. You may catch yourself daydreaming about flirting with that incredibly hot man you encounter on a regular basis, or getting wet at the thought of someone touching you with the lust and desire of passion you're lacking in your life right now. My advice to you is this: it's okay to want those things! It's okay to explore who you are and what you want! Why do you feel like you "could never do that to your marriage" or that it's just "not something good little Christian girls are allowed to do?" My marriage has become stronger because of the level of trust and communication we are now required to have with each other!

Here's my disclaimer: this only works if you are both willing to sit down and have an honest conversation. Let's face it ladies, few men will say, "No honey, I don't want to have sex with any other hot women." If a man says that, he's typically only saying it because he's worried you'll be jealousy and angry. Own up to those emotions if you feel them and deal with them. Do not bring drama to the table. If you can't handle it, then don't do it. But if you want to try having an open marriage, go for it! Be happy and explore!

Most people have rules for play in this lifestyle. Some rules are discussed at length and some are unspoken. Individuals involved in the lifestyle should understand what the other person wants and what they do not want. Ideally, both people in a swinging relationship will be on the same page with all rules. Occasionally, they may break a rule whether it is an accident or on purpose because his/her desire took control of the play instead of their mind. Whatever the rules are, both parties should know them as much as possible in advance. A female may run across something during play that she didn't like and decide to discuss it with the man after play. It may or may not be added to the list of rules. A man may decide he does not appreciate when another man does this or that to his woman. This is an example of something that needs to be discussed after play if he felt like he didn't like it during play. The ONLY way this type of relationship works is if everyone is completely honest and communicates well. If you are fortunate enough to have this relationship, listen to the other person. If they say something bothers them, don't just blow it off. It may not bother you, but it did bother that person enough for them to form the courage enough to tell you they weren't comfortable with it. Listen to their side and work through it!

"I just don't understand how you can do that!" On the off chance my husband and I tell anyone outside of the lifestyle that we enjoy such hedonistic activities, this is the most common reaction we receive. They don't understand how we can be the best sexually and still want others. Or, how either of us can be okay with our spouse going off to meet someone else to play. I think when you boil it down; the person is worrying about feelings developing between their spouse and the other people they enjoy in the lifestyle. Also, they worry about their spouse's safety.

So, what turns you on about a man or woman? Have you ever really thought about it? I know exactly what makes my panties wet! I'm very selective. And when I say very selective, I mean people are surprised I ever indulge in the excitement of this lifestyle after reading my list of requirements! Yes, you did read that correctly – "list of requirements." I know what I want and I'm definitely not afraid to go after it! I won't settle for anything that falls short of my requirements! Literally, I don't do short in either implied sense of the term!

I love the business executive type that can give off a chill, laid back vibe. Clean cut, yet rugged. Polished, yet rough. I also think there's nothing like a sexy black man with a professional career, the manners of a respectable southern gentleman, and a nice, long, thick cock. Those men make me weak in an instant! I try to be professional. I try to keep my demeanor outgoing, professional, and sophisticated. But, apparently, I give off an elusively seductive aura. Men pick up on this vibe and know I play. They pick up on the little cues. They flirt. They test the waters to see if the beautiful ring on my finger matters to me or if I'm willing to explore a little fun with them. I'm good at keeping a straight face and playing things straight laced. But every once in a while, I am drawn to someone. It literally feels like a magnet. I feel that playful personality I have take over me. I'm drawn to how men find reasons to do those sexy little touches on my arm or walk behind me and "accidentally" rub their cock against my ass....Mmmm fuck! I become paralyzed in steamy, mesmerizing stares.

We both eye fuck the hell out of each other. These men create opportunities to give me their number in front of a large group. The best ones like to play with fire. They tempt fate. They purposely flirt right in front of their boring, sweet, holier-than-thou wives. I enjoy this type of man most.

For any man interested in playing with me, you need to meet the following standards:

• You need to be described as attractive, hot, and sexy. I'm attracted to tall, muscular types. You can thank Samson for this requirement!

• Your cock needs to be at least 7"in length and have a bit of width to it. I prefer much larger, but the minimum is seven glorious inches. To men with pencil thin dicks, please do not apply!

• You must be successful at whatever you do. I enjoy an attractive man discussing something he's passionate about.

• I want an intelligent man. I like someone that can carry on a stimulating conversation and challenge me in every way possible! Capturing my mind with dirty, creative thoughts and potential sexy scenes is the fastest way to make me a naughty slut for you.

• I want a gentleman. You may be smacking my ass and talking dirty to me, but you better have some underlying manners mixed in there somewhere! Respect me. Let me know I can trust you and that my safety comes first! Only then will I be open to discussing the option of playing.

• Confidence is also a must! In my opinion, this is the sexiest quality a man can have. Especially if he's Dominant … Mmmm!

Don't get me wrong, every once in a while I get in the mood for true Big Black Cock. I love the feeling of being a filthy cumslut that enjoys sitting on huge, pussy-splitting, dark meat. I am filled with lust while I'm letting him ram it into me until he is finished. Brands are another thing I love on a man. A sexy, young, built, BBC with a brand anywhere near me is an ultimate test in self-control. I want him. I need him. Please understand that I'm focused entirely on getting his cock inside me. I'm slightly obsessed with the contrast of a black dick sliding every inch into my white opening.

When I was a teenager, I had an innate desire to kiss a girl and play with large, supple boobs. I didn't consider actually licking a woman's pussy or having sex with a woman until my husband and I started swinging.

For any woman interested in playing with me, you'll need to meet these standards:

• You must have big boobs. Sorry. I know that may sound superficial. But, so what? That's what I like! I enjoy burying my face in a nice rack. Sucking on her nipples, flicking the tip with my tongue, and hearing her moan when I gently bite down to nibble on them makes me wet. Yeah, I'm all about it!

• I prefer redheads and brunettes.

• Feisty. I need feisty women. I HATE being bored. We can do sweet and sensual, but we better be doing some hair pulling and ass smacking while we're playing too!

• Intelligence is required in order to have a stimulating conversation

• She should be described by those that know her as sexy, but not slutty.

• Beautiful face, curvy body, and confident personality!

• I have a preference for the high maintenance look.

Everyone:

You need to be clean in every sense of the word. Good hygiene is important people! Please take a shower before you play! You must have all your teeth, brush them regularly, and make sure your hair isn't a mess! Disease and drug free is required! I'm not into playing the "guess your disease" game with potential playmates, so you need to have a completely clean test. And yes, I expect you to be tested.

You need to be confident. This is a big one. You can't fake being confident. I read people well. I'll know your strengths and weaknesses within five minutes. I'll know if you're too vanilla for me, a fun playmate, or into bdsm. Would you be a good Dom/Domme, sub, or switch? Don't worry. I already know. You may not. You may not even know what those terms mean. But, I analyze everyone constantly. I know what you think and how you will react in certain situations. In essence, I may be placing my trust in you if you become a playmate of mine. If I may trust my life to you, you better be damn sure I will know you inside and out before we do anything.

Now, after reading all of this can you believe a past

boyfriend dumped me because I was too much of a "goody two shoes?"He dumped me because I wouldn't fuck him. My ex-boyfriend would be able to fuck me anytime now!

CHAPTER 3

Mmmm fuck! The fireman I play with just sent me a message. This man is solid muscle and can make me sore for days. He's rough, sexy, and very confident. While we message, he sends me pictures of his cock and tells me how amazing it feels when I suck him. He wants me to meet him. He wants to feel how wet he makes me every time he shoves his cock in deep. I agree to meet him at an area hotel and when he knocks on the door my heart races. I let him in wearing nothing but a smile. Seeing the lust in his eyes makes me fully aware I'll be flat on my back within seconds. True to form, he slammed the door shut. I smirked and his clothes were off in record time. His cock was already hard; pointing straight at the juicy V it wants. He kisses me, and then pushes me back onto the bed. His hands slide between my thighs and moans into my mouth as his fingers slide into my moist slit. He climbs up over me and teases my opening with the tip of his cock. I want it! He slowly enters me and doesn't stop until he's balls deep inside me. He moves his face to my neck and I feel his lips kiss me before he bites a little. I clench my pussy around his cock, which only causes him to thrust deeper. He picks up speed. The primal need to fertilize my womb takes over him. I tell him I want to suck his cock with my juices all over it. I know a change of pace will make him last longer. I jump up so that he can lie on his back while I savor my taste. I really do love the sweetness. Next thing I hear is, "mmm fuck baby, you have to stop if you don't want it all down your throat." I giggle and move to the side. I get up on all fours, wiggle my ass at him, and tell him I want it rough. This man definitely knows how to give it rough! He grabs my hair and twists it around his wrist, pulling tight. The other hand was pushing his entire weight into my lower back. That makes me arch my ass up even higher like a whore. He hits deeper inside me. He's hitting it so fast that I cum twice before he unloads his seed deep into my cervix. He takes a pic of his cum dripping out of me. He wants to save it on his phone so that he can look at it any time he needs my pussy. The sexy fireman texts me the picture and I send the pic to my husband while he was at work. I also text my husband the name of the hotel I'm playing in and the room number. Within 10 minutes, my husband's cock is between my thighs filling me up too!

So, did you notice I called him "the fireman" earlier? I give all my playmates nicknames. I only remember someone's real name if they were really good! There aren't very many worth playing with a second time. One guy I referred to by an incorrect name for over a year! I didn't call him by the wrong name to his face of course, but I did in my conversations about play with my husband and Dom. We all have very limited amounts of space in our memory. I don't want to jam mine up with specifics I will never need to remember again anyway! It is much easier to assign a nickname related to the person's specific occupation, favorite hobby, favorite travel destination, hometown, or distinguishing characteristic. I know those items of information anyway, so essentially it's the old "two birds with one stone" adage. I'm analytical. I like statistics. I want to track everything. I keep track of how many people I fuck in the notes section of my smartphone. The note reminds me of my number. I only increase the number when I've played with someone new. If I fuck someone I've played with before, the number does not increase. Before I started playing as a HotWife without my husband, I could count how many partners I had fucked on one hand. I was nervous to play alone behind closed doors with another man. All the safety concerns that I could ever possibly have ran through my mind. But when you look at my number today, you'll realize I have gotten over that! I'm very still cautious. I'm still aware. But, I enjoy myself. If I hadn't done that, I would have easily forgotten how many different people I've enjoyed over the last four and a half years. Let's just say that it's gone from being able to count them all on one hand to being into triple digits – in four and a half years! That's me being very picky in the selection of my playmates and working around a hectic work and family schedule! I don't play every time I have the opportunity. I keep my priorities in check. However, my number may make you think otherwise. So, that being said, what's your number? ;) How many people do you want to fuck right now? It's okay. Imagine having this conversation with your closest girlfriend. She can keep a secret. How many other men have you caught yourself wanting? You don't need permission! As long as you're careful and discreet, it's possible to have a successful career, spotless image, and beautiful perfect family. You can do all of that all while being a kinky slut!

I meet up with my Dom to play. At this time, we've known each other about a year. We fuck hard like we usually do, but this time it's a little different. He gets into position he knows I love. He's the only man that fucks me this way! It feels perfect. I get to see his handsome, sexy, dominant face while he's over me with his cock hitting my Gspot perfectly. He has me whimpering for him. I beg him to let me cum. I don't beg anyone for anything, yet I just heard it come out of my own mouth. I have one hand playing with my nipple and the other rubbing furiously on my clit. "Oh my God Daddyyyyy, I'm going to cum!" As soon as the words came out of my mouth, he let out a masculine growl and filled me full of his seed. I'm very thankful I made the decision to get fixed so that we could play bareback! My husband and I are finished having children, so we both got fixed. This way, we stay safe and have fun. Now back to the story. My lover goes to shower. After he gets dressed, he stares at me. Literally, he just stands there and stares! He doesn't normally do that. Normally he showers, gets dressed, gives me a kiss, and leaves. So, why is he staring? I smile and say, "What, baby?" He says, "It's getting harder and harder to leave you." I feel my face blush a little and my pulse race. It's getting harder for me to see him walk out the door each time, too. I just never said it. I gesture for him to come kiss me, a little longer this time than normal, and off he goes. Although he will never admit it, I think he was initially more emotionally invested than I was in this connection we share. Or, maybe I was in denial. It started out as a NSA FWB only kind of situation. And, now there's definitely attachment forming between us. Lord help us!

Let's go ahead and get the touchy subject out of wives and girlfriends out of the way. Let me be clear. I swore I would never play with a married man unless his wife was playing as well. Married people were off limits. Karma is a bitch and I didn't want any negative Karma in my own marriage. So, a rule of mine was that I wouldn't play with any married people that aren't playing together as a couple. That was the rule. Then, I met him. Samson. I even fought against it. Multiple times. I said no to meeting him quite a bit. My husband knew that I would be into this man if I would just give him a chance. God help me! This man is my biggest weakness in life, yet one of my biggest strengths and supporters. I am blessed and beyond content to have this man to share myself with. It sounds odd, doesn't it? How blessed I am to share myself with another woman's man? I'm sure all the married ladies are ready to burn me at the stake after reading that line! But, think about it. No one gets in your marriage unless someone lets that person in your marriage. If someone is in your marriage, your enemy is the person you married. It's the one that made those vows to you and promised to love you. I'm not your issue. The fact your husband is looking elsewhere for pleasure without telling you is the problem. I'm actually very respectful of his wife and child. He is respectful of my family. Content and bliss are words I never imagined I would associate with myself. I'm just not made like that. I always want new, better, bigger, etc. With my husband Seth and lover Samson, I've learned who I really am. I've learned what my personal brand of being content looks like.

CHAPTER 4

"The other woman" – what a label! I have witnessed every woman in my family go through the drama of her husband cheating. All of them! I refused to let that happen to me. That's why I refused to fuck a married man. We were all conservative Christian bible toting, perfect families. Yet, it still happened. So, don't think your family is any different or judge anyone else. And, what's this other stuff? I have no intention of holding any significant meaning in anyone's life other than for my husband and children. There should be no reason to have this title attached to my perfect persona. Except, it happened. I am that woman. And, God help me, I'm not giving it up!

His wife – I feel bad. I'm not this type of person. His wife refuses to be open about playing at all, ever. She's not boring in bed. She's not a dominatrix or anything, but I wouldn't consider her ugly or boring. Honestly, I would not want a playmate that would settle for anyone boring. She's "above average" as he puts it, has a decent job, and what sounds like a protective, loving family support structure. I knew he was married. I found out they have a child. I felt like a trashy slut who is taking their husband or dad away from them for a few hours every once in a while simply because we want each other. Feelings were never an option. I don't do feelings. But, it happened. Oh my God! I've literally become every single thing I swore I wouldn't! I'm the woman that another man messages during the day while he's at work, or sneaks to message while he's at home with his family. Little things remind us of each other, which takes time from her. I'm fully aware of that. I make sure I put what I would assume her wants and needs are above any potential playtime. If it's storming, he should be home with his wife and young child, not meeting me when he gets off work. I wanted to feel his hands all over me, more than just about anything, but not more than his overall happiness in life. That happiness is his wife. My job is to be respectful of their marriage. He's ultimately hers. I was completely fine with that when I was only a swinger and playing with him. When feelings developed, the line blurred. When BDSM, Dom, Domme, sub, and switch roles were added, the line turned into sand on a windy day. It's still there, but damn sometimes it's hard to see it clearly! His wife knows something isn't right. I think most women can feel when their husband is playing behind her back. He's good, but no one's perfect at covering up an affair. She makes up reasons to throw a curveball in plans our plans. Little does she know I'm not going anywhere! He's hers, right? She's got the ring and I think that's wonderful! But, I'm his owner. I'm his Domme. We're lovers through and through. I'm also blissfully happy being his obedient submissive pet. He's mine, too! I'm very protective of this man that I now love.

Now, you may be asking how I find my playmates. There isn't just one way. If you're interested in exploring the lifestyles of swinging, playing around, BDSM, or having an affair, there are some important things you need to know. First, set up a fake email address that doesn't connect back to any other email address you currently use. Second, decide what you want! Do you want a super casual hookup here and there, an affair, someone to enjoy the BDSM lifestyle with, or other people to enjoy for swinging fun? Only you can decide what you want and what you are interested in trying within the lifestyle. The next step is to go online through private or hidden windows on your phone or computer and research! You need to know that "atm" doesn't always stand for someone getting money out of a machine! It can also stand for at the moment, or something else. Finally, search for websites that cater to your interest(s) and see if any allow you to sign up for free. If so, make a free account using the new sexy email address that you just created. You will need to fill out your profile. Less is more when you're completing a profile. Type some accurate, but sexy information in there and attach one photo of a body part that is not immediately recognizable by everyone you know. It doesn't have to be X rated either. Usually a photo of your lips will work well for a profile picture. Do not upload a photo of your wedding rings, piercings, tattoos, birthmarks, specialized nail designs, specific jewelry, or anything else someone would easily recognize as being part of you. You'll start getting emails and instant messages within a day or two, sometimes sooner! Never give out personal information. Never meet someone in a private, secluded place. Be safe! I advise meeting someone once in a semi-public location. You will have a bit of privacy, but you're able to get help if you need it. If you don't need it and you two hit it off, you're still able to chat and get to know each other. One rule of mine is that I do not talk about sex within earshot of anyone I meet in public. People hear things and tell other people. This is the worst form of gossip and you don't need someone hearing how you like to be spanked if you're trying to be discreet! If you want to be successful at this lifestyle, you need to be very observant at all times of who is around you, what you say, what you do, what type of photos you post, etc. Set up a messenger account to allow yourself a way to speak to people without giving out your cell phone number. I made that error in the beginning and wish I hadn't! I still have people I never met in person that text me years later! The last piece of advice is to identify a buddy you can trust. This needs to be someone that you can check in with. They need to know exactly where you're going, exactly who you're with, what you're wearing, and when you'll be back home. When you get home, tell them you're home. Someone needs to know your secret, but it only needs to be one person that can keep their mouth shut and your safety as their number one priority! With all that being said, think about what you want. Do you want a lover? Do you want raw, rough, uninhibited, casual sex? Do you want to explore BDSM? Take the time needed to understand you and your wants. Then, research those wants and start exploring. I'd be happy to recommend a few key websites that I enjoy! If someone is pushy about meeting, take that as a major red flag and move on immediately. Stay safe!

There are other ways to meet men, too. I flirt with men in public when I know it's safe to do so. Men flirt with me. If this happens to you, pay attention to these flirtatious exchanges! These can lead to that person becoming your next playmate. If you encounter a man that would not be good at being discreet, don't start anything with him! There are a few flirtatious men that I've encountered who would not make ideal playmates because of this even though I would enjoy giving them a test drive. We enjoy conversation when we run into each other, but that's it. There is a major website that everyone goes to for everything. Yes, I've used it to search for playmates. I love having current playmates suggest me to one of their friends. They know me well. They know what I'm into and what I don't like. They know what I expect from my playmates. Current playmates frequently message trying to get me to play with someone or suggest a sexy man to me. It is similar to checking references when you're hiring someone. They are my reference check on the person before I ever consider playing with him or her!

As I am typing this, a message pops up from "The Curve." I have a playmate I'll call "T" that is well endowed. The curve of his cock is perfect. He wasn't too thick or too thin. The curve hit my g spot perfectly! T taught me how to ride. He taught me the importance of men being protective of their women, how to be more sociable at a party, and how to be an exhibitionist. My preconceived notion of people that went to a club or parties was that they are trashy. I also thought people that fucked 8 or more people in their lifetime were disgusting sluts. Oh, how things have changed! I went to a swinger's party with T. During the party, he leads me into a playroom. He sits on the couch and has me straddling that cock I have grown to enjoy so much. We are the only ones in the room. Then, I hear a group of people talking on their way in the door. I stop in mid-bounce. I begin adjusting to get off and leave the room when he grabs my hips. T rams his cock into me and shoves my hips down hard at the same time. There is no way in hell he is going to let me leave. He wants to show off. T is almost 7' tall and so incredibly strong that I am always firmly planted onto his lap. He makes me ride until I have cum oozing inside me. I am nervous, self conscious, and incredibly aroused. The rush of feeling 8 sets of eyes watching me is incredibly intense. It feels like they are staring through me! I hear all conversation going on in the room come to a complete stop. I am in the zone and my pussy is dripping wet. I perform my first show for these strangers and after I finish, I have multiple people asking to be next!

T and I have also been on a few out of town trips together. The first time we go out of town, T is kind enough to play bodyguard for me. I want to meet a guy I think will be a good fuck, but I don't want to drive an hour and a half by myself to meet someone that may potentially kidnap or kill me. So, he stays with me the entire time we are in this city. The guy arrives at the hotel room while I'm in the shower. T opens the door and makes idle chit chat before I join them in the bedroom. The guy and I play while my sexy, tall playmate watches. T would make sexy comments here and there about how I like certain things and the naughty, successful engineer fucking me tries to up his game with every comment. Intelligence is very sexy to me and this man is highly intelligent. However, he isn't highly skilled in bed. T shows him to the door and walks over to me. I am lying on my stomach when I feel his hand run up the back of my thigh, over my ass, and up to my hair. He said, "Baby, do you want me to fuck you how you like to be fucked now?" He knew the engineer didn't completely satisfy me. T can definitely satisfy me! I am never able keep track of how many times T can make me cum during our play sessions, but it was easy with the engineer. T fucks me how I need to be fucked. He fucks me raw, hard, and deep. With my pussy full of cum and my insatiable hunger for sex soothed for the time being, we put our clothes on and left to go to a nice Italian restaurant for dinner. I decide not to clean up, so I have my own cum oozing out of me and down my thighs. I look like a sweet, young, professional Banana Republic type. However, he and I both know I am a dirty cumslut that needs to be fucked hard and often.

I message my Dom that evening. "Hello Daddy!" To be honest, the additional sessions are kind of a blur… T used 4 or 5 condoms and he came twice, which was great. We talk about how I should get fixed and how it would give me the option of playing without the risk of getting pregnant. He wants it bareback so bad! I can tell it drives him crazy! I realize I've found his weakness to exploit. If I want him to cum, that's the card I'm pulling. And, I do! :) It works like magic…Mmmm. He thrusts harder and deeper both times I've pulled the "mmm fill me up" card. Yum! He makes me ride him reverse cowgirl and it's fantastic. New positions. He tells me he's not taking no for an answer. We play twice before we go to dinner and two times that night. He sees my phone light up a few times with messages from other men. He's chatting a little with a few women. We search a swinger's website together. After dinner, he's a little rougher. I have scratches all down my back. They're burning as if his nails cut into me. I love it. He blows cold air across them and it feels amazing. We are both lying on our sides when he starts biting my shoulders. When he's over me, he grabs my tits so hard!

He's so strong that I am immediately bruised. He said he didn't mean to hurt me that bad and I tell him it's ok because I like seeing the bruises. He runs with that saying how he likes sending me home with marks. Once, he was on me when you messaged. He asked who just sent the message on my phone. I said, "Oh, that's my Dom." He was all about that. He wants me to talk to you. I tell him that you can wait since you haven't talked to me in days. It's what you deserve. He wasn't having that. I had to make him quit hitting it just so I could see what your message. He even sent one of the pics of us playing to you. I believe he likes riling you up! He knows your place. He never acts jealous and knows that I want to talk to you. He's very respectful. But, I think he still wanted to show you his role. I call my husband between playing and check on the kids. He asks if I am having fun and I say "Yeah, right now actually." I ran through a very, very short summary of the engineer and I saw T smiling. I kiss him and stroke his cock while I talk to my husband, but my husband cannot hear it. At least I don't think he can - I try to be quiet. Mmmm… Maybe I can get use to the idea of a boyfriend.

I'm not sure if that's all of the story or not. I'm sure I'll remember other things that I forgot. I promised to be honest and maybe this email is for nothing more than to clear the thought out of my mind. But being as honest as I can let myself be with you, when I got back into bed it was nice having T with me. I kick my husband out of bed every night because he snores like a fucking freight train and I have to sleep sometime. I miss having a man there beside me. I was not worried for my safety at all because he's a perfect gentleman when he's supposed to be a gentleman. I caught myself thinking of you. I wanted you there! What would be different? What would you have been like sitting there watching the engineer fuck your submissive? Would you make the same comments? Would you join me and give me what I want or just let the guy do his thing? Would you would have teased the person at the front desk that called telling them that, "the room is fine but the dude needs to step it the fuck up from good to pushing me if he plans on pleasing your pet." Or messing with the older lady we had as the waitress by putting me in an awkward situation saying something like "Your husband won't appreciate all the bruises I'm putting all over you." Would I have let you sleep at all? I probably wouldn't have let you sleep. I wouldn't be nervous about my safety or too worried about sleeping in front of you. I like that you're the one that can read me, push me, know my limits, and who pushes me hard. I need that from someone. I love playing with fire and I think you could be perfect for that.

But, then I hear my husband's seemingly new favorite phrase when we talk about you - he's just talk. You had the opportunity to have me overnight and you didn't take it. You could brand or pierce or cut, but you haven't. I even buck him on no condom, which he hates. But, I love playing with fire. He knows the risks as well as we do. But, he doesn't want a kid and truthfully that's a valid concern I have as well. He hasn't said it, but it seems like he's taking rules down and allowing more because he's testing you. He wants to show he's right. Damn it! I always hate when he's right about anything. There are times I'm playing when someone does something that makes me think of you. It does seem one sided. Damn him for being right.

So then I'm stuck. And in that situation, that makes me wiggle my ass against T's cock. He wakes long enough

to kiss me and give me a gentle hug. I do like playing…
not with many, but enough to keep up with the amount
of sex I want. If that's just my husband, then I'm totally
fine with that. I'm purely driven by want and need. Can
I control it? Yes. Do I want to? No fucking way! If I
don't have to, I'm not controlling anything. I'm learning
to enjoy the moment I'm in when it's convenient to do
so, or when I don't want to take the time to think. No
reason to analyze when I'm getting what I want at the
time. I'm plain and simple. I'll tell you anything you
want to know - good or bad - whether I want to or not.
If I have hard rules, then that's one thing. If I don't,
then I want to be pushed as far as I can!
Mmmmmmmmmmm…

T is a sexy single man that I ended up making a regular
playmate. I visited his house very frequently and stayed
over many times. I fell asleep after he kissed me and
said, "Goodnight, baby." We went on trips out of state
to sexy swinger parties, again, causing us to stay
overnight with each other. My husband isn't the party
type, so he loved hearing the stories. We would send
him sexy pictures of how I was dressed, my slit oozing
cum, his cock in me, and my face when he was

thrusting that massive cock in me.

My husband and I eat dinner with our entire family. We are fun, chill, laid back, and enjoy anything funny! We take turns giving each other an hour or two here and there for play, so don't think he's missing out! He's played with some sexy women too! There's only been one I seriously had an issue with. She was headstrong, wanted what she wanted, when she wanted it, how she wanted it. My husband is not a beck and call person. I don't know who she thinks she is, but I'm the only Domme here. She needs a single guy with nothing better to do than be right there for her any second she needs him. Is she pretty? Yes. Is she hot? Ummm… no. We have a life, responsibilities, and family. Sorry, you need to find another sucker because it won't be my husband. I'm protective of my perfect life! But, any time you want him to fuck you for a quick hour or so, let him know. So, my husband and I end up having a fight over this chick. I remember sitting at a public water park with him after a day of arguing about how he was going to go see her whether I liked it or not. I'm sorry, when did her needs trump the needs of his wife and his children? Yeah. It was a rough day. So, the next day we are at the water park and I just want to soak up the sun. I'm still pissed and he obviously is too. Something starts it all over again and I've been chatting with my lover off and on through all of it. I will remember this conversation like it was yesterday no matter how old I get. I told him, "Maybe I'd be better off single. He can go do whatever it is he wants whenever he wants because that seems to be more important than me. I will be fine with work, school, my kids, and I'll play here and there." He says, "You can't be single." I almost get defensive thinking he was going to say I'm the type of woman that always has to be attached to a man. I most certainly am not and I can take care of my children and myself! Instead I exercise patience and say, "Why not?" My lover's next message pops up on my screen. It says, "Because I'd fall in love." I stop completely and just stare at my phone. Did he really just type that? I reply that I don't have to be single for that to happen and I get two words back from him, "I know!" We hadn't discussed the L word, or feelings too much for that matter. We both knew they were there, but that's it. We don't cuddle after playing or anything because I refuse to cuddle and make connections. But, there it was. I dig deeper and long story short, I end up with the feeling that it's too late for him. He's fallen. Is it a temporary, rose-colored glasses situation? I don't think so.

Now, almost five years after we met, he says he does love me. But, he will not say those three exact words to me. It's painful and even infuriating at times, making me feel as if I'm nothing more than just some girl he graces with his presence when he has nothing better to do. I know that's not true, but it's hard to wrap your head around it sometimes. The invisible line gets blurred. After all the conversations about how if he were single I'd be at his house, what we'd be doing, how I'd have things there - it's very blurry. I do respect that he doesn't say it and that he reserves that only for his wife. I also believe it is possible to love more than one person in this lifetime. You see people do it all the time. That doesn't mean I love my husband any less, it just means that I'm becoming more content. I want nothing more than for their marriage to be happy and solid. My only request that we spend a little more time together than we get. We're both very busy people, so we don't have much time anyway. I knew I was in for a rollercoaster the first time his wife caught him messaging some other woman. It was very soon after the first time we played. He and I were messaging that day. We were very casual then, with no attachment at all. We didn't chat every day. Then, all of a sudden he messages that he has to go and he doesn't know when he will be able to get back in touch with me. What the fuck?! We were joking around two minutes before that and then all of a sudden I get the message that he has to go and may not be able to speak to you again. What happened? As it turns out, his wife caught him messaging some other woman and got pissed. It wasn't me. I was like a zombie. I didn't know what had just come over me, but it wasn't healthy. For the next six weeks, I was in a really dark place. I cried a lot. I didn't eat much. I didn't talk to many people or go to any events. I didn't know what had just happened to me, but I knew I couldn't get out of the horrible place I was in. Then I realized it was because he left. I had zero, maybe even negative, attachment to him before. He was amazing, but we were both clear we weren't looking to screw up our marriages. So, why was I so upset? He apparently meant a lot more to me than I realized. Six months after meeting him, I knew he owned me.

Then a couple of weeks after that, my husband and I are laying in bed watching TV. I'm messaging my Dom that morning and then he's offline for a bit. We discuss him while we're watching TV. My husband says very bluntly, "It's because you love him." I couldn't believe what I was hearing. That was a rough weekend at my house. He was very kind about it and I spent most of the weekend crying. I felt like I had failed my husband. I felt like the words weren't true, but I knew deep down they were. There was a lot of soul searching that weekend and ultimately, my husband was right.

CHAPTER 5

Now, let's get to the good stuff!

I've played with women. Quite a few women actually! I enjoy their softness mixed with a fun, feisty personality. Women also like to take more photos during play, so I enjoy that! I love looking back at photos of my sexual encounters. Now, on to couples! I've played with so many couples! Couples, let me be clear. You're not my favorite, so I usually try to avoid you. The woman tends to get jealous and then I don't have any fun. However, some couples have been awesome! One of the first couples my husband and I played with were fun, chill and we played with them until 4:00 a.m. the next morning when we were just suppose to meet quickly for what I call a "just meet" at 7:30 p.m. That evening, we had an entire gallery of photos taken, the man from the other couple directed play, and it was the first time I had licked a woman. She said I was a natural! And, her pussy is still my favorite! On another night, that same couple had me all to themselves. I ended up with the girl wearing a strapon fucking me while on her knees in front of me. I was on the couch with my legs open wide. Her husband was behind her fucking her. So every time he hit hard into her, she would hit hard into me. It felt incredible! After that, I got down in the floor on all fours. She decided to lay under me and we played a fun game of 69 for a bit until her massive dicked husband entered me. With him being a rough dominant type fucking me while she was licking my clit, I experienced one of the best orgasms I'd ever had! I have so many stories that there's no way to include them all!

Ok, so England is out of town again. I passed on going with him - partly because I had to work, partly because I just met him once. I text him while he's gone and he gives me his availability for his first two days he's back. I text at work Friday and we're scheduled for Saturday at 1. I have to plan around my husband's 3:00, which later changes to that morning before mine. I ask for his address and tell him I'll be sending it to my husband just in case. I ask where his wife will be and he said he'd get her to take the kids out. The next text says that he just talked to her and she's staying to eat me. Omg. I said that I'd prefer just him the first time. He joked that he had to take advantage of the situation. Normal events for the morning and he says his sitter situation is falling apart so he only has until 2:00. I'm good with that because that's within my hour. He asks if I can come earlier so we'll have longer. I was pretty close, so I agreed. Showing up 15-20 minutes early, he opened the door before I even got there. Nice house. There was a drawing made by one of his kids on the front door - super cute. The most attractive quality in a man is that he is a good father to his children —one who really genuinely enjoys spending time with them having fun, teaching them and being someone they can respect. We say hi and I mention the drawing. He explains and we kiss. Best thing about England as we call him, or as you know him 100+, is that he can kiss very well. I still can't believe he's fucked over 100 people. What a slut! So, he has to be amazing in bed, right? The decor of the office and other rooms I can see from the entry match my design taste. Maybe she and I would get along well… Maybe next time…

He goes up ahead of me - that NEVER happens. He's ready. Ok… Let's get started. I walk in to the master and it's typical of what I would expect. But, I'm pleased. He walks over to look out his front window to see if his neighbor has started over to his house, since they know he's home now. The kids are at different people's houses for a little bit and he has football on his television. Seriously? Omg! He slowly walks over never taking his eyes off me and takes my head in his hands. The kiss was great. The goatee is hot. He's older than me, which I usually do not like, but there was something that caught my attention about him. I think it's his confidence in talking about things, his wife, playing in general, and he doesn't care who knows it. I'm really like that. It's refreshing to be around a real person even if I can't be.

He's talking and there's a towel already on the bed. Prepared - love it. I slide my shoes off, socks, jeans, and my sexy blue blouse. I'm left in blue lace panties and pure white Fredrick's bra. I climb on the bed. As soon as I sit, I feel that it's a Tempurpedic. Nice. I prefer my specific brand of snobby mattress brands, but still nice. He climbs on top of me and starts kissing. With one hand he unhooks my bra, whips it off and starts on the bottoms.

I start sucking his cock. Definitely a good size and I'm ready to see what he's learned through all those 100. I make sure I don't scratch too hard, but some. Fun. He tells me how much he wanted me to do that when we met the first time. I told him he didn't ask. He asks about photos and video, but I tell him I don't usually do that. He licks me and has one finger in me. I like that he's respectful, but one isn't going to cut it. Long story short, everything's kind of a blur. He was okay at oral and I was only halfway excited through the time he tried later and I supposedly came both. He's over top of me kissing me again and I feel him press himself against my lips. He asks if I want him to just slip it in and I say no, he has to get a condom. He just says fine and gets one. Not mad, just like yeah I know. But, he tried. At least he gets points for trying. He gets up and comes back with one from the master bath. I was up on my knees and he smacked my ass. "Really? I'm sure you can hit it harder than that" - well challenging him was better... He hit it hard enough to make me wince and my ass was on FIRE! I don't know how many times he spanked my ass on the right, but definitely more than the left side. He hits more on the side than anyone else and I can only guess what shade it is. I can feel the heat radiating off it. I finally have to say, "Ok, you win" and he seems pleased. Glad he never stopped fucking me because I was totally turned on now. I bent straight over with my face on the bed and got it good. He's hitting it pretty hard and then cums quickly. It's deep, feels good, and I'm totally into it. He finishes before I do. Great.

We chill for a few kissing and touching. He tells me to suck him, so I clean it off and do it. He says he'd love just one pic of me doing that. Fine - I'd love to tease my husband anyway. He takes the picture and sends it to my husband too :) He tells me to ride it and I say no. He just says alright. He didn't push at all. I like being respectful of rules, but I don't want a man I can bulldoze either. He's on top of me, my legs are up in the air, and he's grabbing my hair on each side of my head as if it were in pigtails. OMG I hear a little snap and I know I just lost some hair. He's hitting it good now, so I try not to think about it. I cum a couple of times while he's over me. He grabs my boobs hard - like tight gripping and I know there will be a bruise. Sucking hard on the nipple seemed to be what he liked and he was good at it. His necklace is over his mouth and I start playing with it. That's hot. He pulls it in his mouth with his tongue. I sit up and kiss him while he's fucking me. We both cum again and are satisfied. And, neither of us is late! Even better.

After the second time, I start gathering up my stuff and he's getting cleaned up. As we're getting dressed and walking down to the door, we chat. One last long kiss and I'm out the door. He tells me his schedule for the next week or so and I say ok and bye as I'm getting in the car. I look at the time. I call my husband to find out where he is. We meet up and I gasp when I sit down. He smiles and asks if I'm ok. I say yeah, I just need to sit different. We take the kids to the park with my ass still burning in my jeans.

CHAPTER 6

After 100+ my husband and I were able to spend the evening together. We went to dinner. We were completely chill from our play dates. We tried throwing tidbits of information in while we were waiting for a table and more in depth during our meal. As a side note - I was able to chat with this sexy real estate agent that's caught my attention. I told my husband to email his friend that happens to live in the same town as that day's playmate and tell him to bring her up with him next time he comes. His version of bring her up was lame, so I deleted it, retyped it and gave his phone back to him to read for approval. Of course he freaked and said he couldn't send that - I naturally reach over quickly and hit send. I laughed so hard I cried! Little everyday Domme things that push...

We had a fun evening and went back to my parent's house to pick up the kids. While we were out looking at playhouses, I texted my IT guy and set up a play date for Sunday morning. I already had his availability for the next week, so I could pick a day I would want to play. He was going to be huge and I couldn't wait. I always get nervous when someone says they love to do oral on a girl… From what I've experienced, that usually means they're not good at it. We'll see if my theory holds up…

I noticed my doctor was on, so I decided to tempt him. I was in a funny, joking mood - why not? He always just chats when he can and never meets. After about 2 hours of on and off chatting, he was all worked up. Very detailed, confident and straight to the point. We've talked about a lot. We've chatted about things that are exciting; turn ons, turn offs, and especially you.

He's different. He's very hesitant of local play. It took a long time to arrange a meeting right before I changed jobs and that's been it. I knew he likes being Dom. I knew he's very open to trying thing and likes certain things. He wanted someone that he can say to do something and they just do it without question. As long as it's not against my rules… :)

Ok, so I'm sitting at my parent's house and he's messaging. I'm wet, my husband's smiling, and my family has no idea. The whole conversation started out with a message from me saying, "Come fuck me." Long story short, he was very excited and I said that I could stop by and say hi on the way home. He's ready to play the next morning and said that he wasn't going second. I thought I'd mess with him and try to call him out, so I said that he'd probably pick one or the other so I wasn't sure about meeting that night. We stopped to pick up our other vehicle on the way home and I went to meet him at work.

I pull up and he comes out. I try not to watch him walk over because I was already wet. I knew I couldn't handle it. We sit and talk. He seems nervous because he's at work. As soon as he gets in he kisses me. He doesn't kiss. And, he was never willing to compromise that at any point. Ever. He definitely was not willing to at work. He wasn't willing to do a quick kiss either. I definitely had a smile on my face. "Is that what you wanted?" "MMMMMMM Yes," is all I could get out. He picked up my hand and placed it right on his cock. I rubbed it a little and he was so hard. I wanted it. I stop playing and we talked some more. He has the chillest personality - very bohemian. I always try to match my personality to the person I'm around. He's so chill that it's actually difficult for me to be that way.

We run through things I won't do. He explained that he

thought the day he met me that I seemed timid and that was surprising to me. We sent messages that day which apparently got him thinking because they definitely weren't timid. The word he uses is that I "intrigue" him. How funny! I've definitely heard things he likes that I'm willing to do and something he's asked that made me take a step back and have to say no. I play with the string on his scrubs and he's grabbing my boobs. He kisses me again and I love the goatee - which was clean-shaven last time. He's not sure how to read me when I'm playing, if I'm serious or just kidding, so that can be funny. He told me he wanted me to suck it and I said, "huh, imagine that." He just looked at me. LOL. I suck for maybe a minute and he stops me. "Oh baby stop" and he doesn't even remember he's at work. We're talking about one of the biggest swingers clubs in the South that we've both been to and things I'd like to try. I just kiss the tip of it and we start talking again. I tell him how I like to have things decided for me and even micro-managed. He just can't see that because I seem so in control of everything all the time. So we go through all that and how if I say no or it's a rule, it's really a no. Otherwise, it's fair game. He pulls it out and stops playing with my boobs. He has his hands on the back of my headrest and puts it easily on the back of my head. He asks me to suck it again and I get to do it longer. But, I don't do it too long. I taste a little bit of him and I get so excited. He pulls me back off to tease and kisses me. We go back through another conversation before I'm finally able to play. Those eyes and completely calm voice - you just get mesmerized... I did what he really likes and he told me he wanted to cum in my mouth. I said, "imagine that" again. He doesn't get loud or rough or stern... In the same flat tone, he says, "get over here and suck it." I bend over the center console and take it all the way down. As you know, I don't really try the first time, so I just give him average run of the mill sucking. He's moaning and talking dirty...I couldn't believe he could get any harder, but he did. Just as he was telling me he was about to cum, I start doing longer strokes so that I can catch my breath better when I get it. Of course he knows better than that, he puts both hands on my head. At no point was he insanely rough. I pulled up before so that I could catch a big breath, but the suction never leaves. He wasn't having that and he just held me down…. the whole time. He pushed my head up and down from 3/4 down to all the way down and never let me up for a breath. He came forever. It was so much and so hard I could feel the heat shoot up my nose. I had to swallow three times before the last time I was allowed up.

He was completely relaxed. He kept saying as always how I drive him crazy and he loves the differences in control and willingness to experiment. We chat again for about 10 minutes and he checks his phone a couple of minutes into the convo to make sure they didn't call for him. The stethoscope was a turn on… He says bye and tells me that we would meet up in the morning when he gets off. He leaves and I wait for him to get in the building before I leave. I drive home talking to my husband as usual. He messages me and I tell him I have to be up early, so just leave me something. That way I'll know when the alarm goes off if I'm getting ready for our play session or not. I know he's super nervous about meeting in town. He doesn't want to. But, he can't say no. He wants it and he has to have it. But, he can't risk someone seeing him….

I start chatting again and cut that dude off because I

have to be ready for my Dr. if he mans up. With 3 hours of sleep ahead and a guy that likes rough dominate play; I need every minute I can get. I wake 15 minutes before the alarm goes off and he's messaged. He tells me where, when, exactly what to wear and bring with me - I smile and hit snooze twice before heading to the shower...

I start the shower... I need some HOT water to wake up. I'm instructed to wear a short skirt, knee boots, black bra, panties, and a button down shirt. I'm also instructed to bring my favorite toys and ice. I can't believe I'm getting up early again this week for this... but I've waited for this one for so long. I'm not patient. If I don't meet and/or play within a short time frame and the person is local, I'm done. I just don't have time for playing often and I'm not going to spend it chatting with someone that won't meet. There are only two guys that have ever caught my attention enough to wait for - so we'll see if he's worth the wait. I jump in the shower and shave. I fix my hair quickly because I know I'm late. I look through my stuff and I don't have anything black clean. I opt for a compromise - Fredrick's bra: pink with black lace and pink lace panties. Same short Vera

Wang skirt - maybe a new trend for the first with someone... Black button down Ralph Lauren dress shirt with layered ruffles from my neck down the front. I ask my husband to get up and help me pick things out while I'm in the shower and it's all ready for me when I'm done with my hair. I smile looking at him lying in bed. He looks asleep. I ask if he's asleep or even excited at all. Then he shows me and, well, he's very excited :) I get dressed. Walk over to the bed and kiss him bye. I walk through the house quietly, so I don't wake anyone and head to our dining room. I grab my black boots and sit at the table. Slowly I point my toes and slide them all the way up. I pick up my purse and walk out the door.

I message my sexy Doctor all the way there. I didn't get the toys, the undergarments aren't exact, but I do stop for a sweet tea so I'll have ice. He mentioned two hotels the night before, so I drive to the one that's opposite from the one he picked. It was closer and I wanted to beat him there. He wants everything we do to be even more discreet than I do. That's an amazing feat! So, I want to make him chill. I get there early while he's finishing up work. I check in and drive around to the room. I park far away from the door, so that someone driving by wouldn't see it. I didn't realize how far I was going to be walking in high-heeled boots. I walk to the door and a guy is standing by a construction truck. Another is by his door, a couple of doors down. I text my Dom the hotel and room number - got to keep Master happy. I try the key and it lights up red. Ugh! Really? I try the other key the lady gave me and it didn't work either. I try them both again. I try to unlock it quickly with the key and slowly. I tried every way I could think of, but the door would not unlock. In the mean time the dude at the truck says, "Damn, those are some high boots." I said, "yeah, sometimes." He replied, "Oh, so does that mean they aren't always up?" I said not always. He comes over to me and asks if I'm just getting in and I say no. He laughs. I explain I can't get the key to work and of course he offers to help. It won't work for him either even though he's trying to act like he knows how to do it and I don't - if only he knew not to talk to me like that… I cuss and start walking off. He offers to go to the front with me and I say nah, I'm fine. He said he has to go anyway and I decline again while I'm walking back to the car. Shit! Why didn't I park closer? I pull back up in front of the window where the golfers are eating breakfast. I can't tell you how much I hate walking in there dressed like that in a big fur coat to start with - let alone again. I look like a prostitute! I stop at the door and get out. Of course the dude is right there, holding the door open for me. I say thank you because I'm a lady first :) and he says, "You're so beautiful and you won't even say hi to me." I don't even pay any attention to him. I just look at the chick at the front desk and hold my hands up like WTF! She gives me a new set of keys and back around I go. This time, there were three new ones standing outside. GREAT! Where the fuck is he?? I might need the sexy, muscular, tan, tattooed arms of my Dr. to deck these dudes if they get outta line. They start talking to me and it doesn't work again. The golfers are outside the next time I go around. Embarrassing. Guess what, next keys didn't either. I'm so pissed - what happened to discreet? I go back in and I am given a different room. The clerk tells me the lock for the new room will be tricky. The first lock was supposed to be good? Wonderful. My first time up proved to be no different than the first time with the first door. I message him again and he's freaking out. He's almost at the motel when he replied back, "maybe that's a sign." Umm…no, get your ass here. I'm the one going in and out of the lobby. Quit freaking out and get here and fix it. He gets there and tries the door, nope. I go down to get her and she comes to open the door, which of course works after a few times for her. I've been in about 4 times now and I'm past determined that I'm going to fuck him.

He ran down to his truck while she unlocked the door. I messaged him when I got in and he came back up. I had asked him to grab my drink before I went to the lobby and he had brought it back with him. I don't take drinks - anywhere - when I play. Not even around a regular playmate. Someone could put something in my drink. Yeah, I really think about all those silly little things. I wanted to test him…and myself. I open the door and there he was. I shut the door behind him and latched it. He put his stuff on the table before walking to the back of the room. I used the restroom quickly before he came in and he heard the toilet still running for a second. He must have been freaked out because he had to go check it out and see what the sound was.

He says he likes my outfit. I sat on the bed to pull my boots off. He unzips his hoodie. I throw my boots over to the couch and he's staring at me. He walks over to me and I stand up. I kiss him and sit back down. I expect him to naturally push back on me kissing and get started. That would be typical. Not this one. He's standing there staring. Everyone has certain things that they are good at, like to do, don't like… well… this is one of his. He looked straight at me and didn't say anything. It wasn't the sexy playful look of my Dom that makes me want to know what he's thinking and jump him right then. It was completely serious for someone so chill. He said, "Get on your knees." He had said the evening before that he didn't want to scare me by being too Dom while we were messaging and I didn't really know what he could do that would scare me. But, the look must have been part of it. Not like he'd hurt me, but I knew he wasn't playing and you wouldn't want to cross him. He wasn't deep, loud or hateful with his voice. The "opposite" of such a serious look and demand against his tone put me straight down in front of him.

His cock is perfect. Big, not super thick and not thin

(neither of which I like), and rock hard. He tells me to suck it and I don't get to go long. He says, "stand up" and I think I'm up before he finishes saying it. "Take off your shirt," he demands and I start unbuttoning. His scrubs are off quickly and I pull my skirt off. He gets to me before I take anything else off and says, "On the bed on your knees!" Yes sir! Up I go and he slowly pulls the pink lace down my ass. Next thing I know I get a SOLID hit on my right cheek. Not the stinging kind, although it burnt after. It was hard with lots of force behind it. I knew that it would cause a bruise. He went after the left next. It was twice per cheek and the first time was bad. Second, I about gave in. I tensed waiting for the awful hit I was about to get and there wasn't a third. Whew! If there had been a third I would have been crying. Two seconds later his finger was inside me hitting hard. A few minutes later we were at two fingers hitting hard and it felt like knuckles while he was stretching it a little. It felt so good! He's playing with my boob over my bra with his other hand and yanks one side of the bra down so hard that my boob falls out hard. He grabs it and squeezes hard. Ouch! "Take your bra off!" I sit up, unhook it and he's still hitting me hard with his fingers. I lean into him and he grabs me again. I throw it across to the pile of clothes on the couch and he kisses my neck. That's dangerous…mmm… Mental note - I can't tell this one about the spot that drives me crazy wild with lust. He tells me to flip on my back and starts licking. I'm not easy to get off. I could literally make a shopping list or plan out the things I need to do that day while someone is doing that. It's just not my favorite thing. If someone gets me, it's great, but it's not a guaranteed thing. My hot Dr. made me cum twice! He's actually really good and I didn't even have to fake it just to get him off me. Of course, I'd ever do that… :)

He asks where the condoms are and I go get them. He sees one and says that's going to be too small. We'll see… Next command, turn the other direction on the bed (facing the side instead of the headboard) and up on your knees. Two seconds flat and I was facing the other way. He puts it on and slides inside. I'm soaking wet. He's ramming it hard, definitely good at talking and I'm pretty loud. After just a few minutes, we're both enjoying a fantastic orgasm at the exact same time. It is rare and perfect. And, other than Samson, the Dr.

gives the best spankings!

I'm always interested in what the guy does with the condom. That's probably something that people never pay attention to. Little things like that give a good read on a guy…what they're going to be like to play with, how they act, their personality. He yanks it off and throws it on the nightstand. He lies next to me smiling. We kiss and I tell him how good he tastes. He laughs and I explain how it tastes. It was the gum he had been chewing - mmm, yummy. I try to warn people now that after I play I usually leave to get back home. He's the only man other than Samson that knows I'd rather learn to try to make myself stay for even a minute and not feel anxious. I know that's what he's thinking, so we talk. Finally! I get that sexy tattoo I've been thinking about. Tattoos are hot. Sometimes muscles are hot. Usually not something I care about. Definitely not together - I won't even pay attention. The day we first met, he had just been at the gym and I saw the tattoo he said a friend designed for him. That's what caught my attention about him. Those sexy arms with that tattoo… I keep very few pictures anyone ever sends me. I just prefer to delete everything, but the one of his tat is on my phone! :) This is the man that understands discreet, completely NSA, doesn't want to kiss, and now look at him. I must have some effect on men!

He wants me to do what he likes. I ask if he's sure and he says yes. Of course, I remember this conversation from before, so I don't hesitate. It's such an amazing thing to see someone so hot, in control, and successful with everything going for them in their perfect life be so incredibly nervous and concerned. It makes them vulnerable. It's the opposite of how they usually are and that's intoxicating for me. Opposites excite me the most! They are so dominant that I get a high from just playing. Now, seeing this completely other side of watching that person experience something they enjoy. Something most would think is painful. Something I actually enjoy doing even though I'm hesitant. Watching their face - it's such a singular, powerful moment. He was ready to go after a few minutes of that and he told me to stand up. Wtf? Really? I didn't say anything because I was trying to think what I was going to have to do. He said, "Play with your clit." I like being a smartass, so I said, "no." Big mistake. He's not the fun, playful, competition type. I'll remember that. He gave me that same stare. Oh no! I knew I was about to get a punishment and the wait was horrible. Even though it was only a few seconds in reality, it felt like forever. Calmly he reaches up to my right boob, like he's going to play with me just like everyone else in the past. I relaxed half a second and his eyes never changed. I should have known... Before I even realized it, he gripped my nipple hard and twisted it so hard I just knew my nipple had to be in his hand when I finally had to push it away because it was so painful. We didn't say a word during this. After I pushed his hand away, he just flatly said, "Play with your clit." I wasn't about to try him again, so I did as I was told. No joking - check. Got it. He stroked a minute and then told me to suck him. I love hearing him while I do that. Not many are good at that time, but he was. His moans were erotic. I got it harder this time. He pulls me off him and wants to fuck me. He wanted to spank my sexy ass, but I already had solid red marks. He took his time toward the end and I could feel every inch slow and deep. Then, surprised me by ramming it. I screamed and he said to get the pillow. He told me in a conversation the night before he does that. He told me to put my face in the pillow. Pounding full length with me screaming into a pillow he yanks my head up by my hair. I groan when his hands end up on my shoulders and he pushes my back down flat, so that I'm on a sharp angle. Face down, ass up. I tell him how much I love feeling every inch of his cock in me and how I want to feel him cum inside me. On command, he came with me. Wow, round 2 was fun. I'm laying in the curve of his shoulder and he's saying how I drive him crazy and he's having fun fucking me. Very hipster saying… Just as soon as we were finished, I start touching his cock because he's getting me worked up again. He said, "Baby, I need more than 30 seconds. I can go quick but give me a minute." I kissed him and ran my fingernails lightly on his chest. No marks, no scratches. He's married. I can't leave evidence on him of our sexual escapade. Through the play date we mention that we would love to stay there and play all day. He says, "you know, it wouldn't take much to get me hard again." I said, "Imagine that." He said, "Clean it off and suck it." I had finally been conditioned. I didn't hesitate. I lick my palm, run it down the full length and do the same with the other hand. I go straight down on it and we're ready again. He teased way more this time, but again came on cue when I wanted him to. Hair pulling this time was much tighter and I really had some pulled out.

I think the first thing out of his mouth the third time is "You're so hot." You can see him thinking, but he didn't say anything for a minute. I start lightly tracing his tattoo with my fingernail. Perfect. I say that he made me wait long enough and he explains about thinking I was timid the day we met, not having a lot of time in his family and work schedule, not willing to do local play, blah, blah, blah. I hear him and answer, but I'm kissing his tattoo. I've wanted my mouth on it for a while. He asks about my day and if it's going to be busy. I'm satisfied so I plan to cancel the next play date and tell him that I'll be with family all day. He calls me out, knowing I was going to be fucking again. I tell him the other can wait. He said that he likes how I'm experimental and willing to try things. He tells me how good I smell and that he'd smell like me too if he stayed with me. We both said, how he couldn't go home like that. I can feel myself twitching my foot, which is crossed over the other up in the air while I'm lying on my stomach. I'm anxious and want out, but I'm trying my best to stick it out. My Dr. calls me out on wanting to go and reminds me how much fun I would have missed if I had bolted after the first time. True. And, his calm personality helped. Lots of questions and conversation made it easier too. He said, "Ok, you can go now." Funny. I just wasn't ready at the time to be around someone that wanted more than just a quickie, let alone a dominant that could actually be pretty perfect for me. He just wasn't MINE. I wasn't prepared to understand how to play with two dominant people at the time and I wasn't risking what I had with my Dom for anything.

Somewhere during the session, he sucked by boobs hard. So hard they were pulled all the way up from my body while I was lying on my back. He sucked so hard I thought he was biting my nipple. The hot doctor rubbed his cock on my opening like he just wanted to push it in and paid attention to my ass, but never tried anything because he knew it was part of my Dom's rules. I don't really remember where these things fit, but they were in there somewhere…

I start getting dressed and he takes a shower. I wanted to shower with him, but I knew we'd end up fucking again and I was out of condoms. Although, he is fixed! :) He offers me a piece of gum and I gladly accept. He's dressing and we're chatting about our kids and how they have practice so many nights a week with sports and his impossible work schedule that was part of keeping him away so long, where he lives, family, etc. He hands me cash for the room and there was something sexy about the exchange… He hangs out in the room and I go check out. I get a message from him a little bit later saying he had fun, etc. I know he was nervous and is still nervous. If we play again, I'll be surprised. He'll have to get out of his own head and just do it…again.

I call my husband to recap and he talks me into my next appointment…

CHAPTER 7

This guy and I have met up once. He's good at sexy conversation. He's a good kisser. This guy is 6' 8" and now I seem to go for taller. The problem is that I hate the cutesy little name he calls me. It's one of those southern sweet names like honey, sweetie, doll, honey, etc. Blah! He's very outgoing. We've chatted on and off forever. We just met him within the last couple of months. I suppose I've put him off long enough. The cutesy stuff kept me away.

I'm driving around with my husband and think "he said he's free some this weekend, let's just see." Not married. Good dad. Attractive. A fan of the same football team I am (hey that's important in the South!). These are good attributes in a man! We're texting and he's free for Sunday morning around 10. The play date is set for his parent's house while they're outta town. It's a nice home near a golf course. He's doing a great job of flirting with me through texts and I forgot how big he was. Why, yes…I believe we will meet :)

I text him at 9:00 a.m. like I told him I would to tell him I'm already in town. He says he's getting outa the shower and will let me know when to head on over. I go sit at one spot for a while talking to my husband and then go wash my car. He texts that he's there, so I can come over whenever. He said the garage is open and to come through that way. I'm a little earlier than 10:00, so he'll have extra time. Crap.

I see a luxury sports car in the garage. His SUV is out in front. I look down and see the fancy finish on the driveway that's really too small to waste the money on it. He opens the door with a sexy greeting. When I get to the door, we hug and kiss. I use the bathroom to freshen up, and then wander through the house until I find him. I place my purse on the dining room table and he wraps his arms around me with a huge kiss. Mmmm! I can't think when I'm kissed well. And, who would really want to?

He shows me which way to go and suggests that I go first. That's so typical. I make small talk about things in the house on the journey and he's watching my ass all the way up the steps. I stop at the top of the stairs because I don't know which room to go in. He points letting me know which one we will be using and I walk in. I see a toy gun on the bed and I think of my sexy

Dom and the gun conversations we've had. I ask if we'll be playing guns. He answered, but I was actually thinking about someone else! :) I sit down, pull the boots off and we kiss. It seems like a pattern... Not that I'm complaining because he can kiss well.

The next hour or so was spent with him licking me and getting me off about 4 times. I kept thinking he's good at it, but once I've cum like that one time, it's really easy to get me again and quickly... So, is he that good or is it because of the Doctor I just fucked? I'm thinking and playing - not a good sign. We tried every position possible and he was so thick. He stretched me and I had to stop him in one position because it hurt too much. I sucked so much my jaw hurt. He kept taking breaks because he was tired. He would wash his cock after each magnum and have me suck it again. He would actually go all the way into the bathroom and wash it. Our mouths were completely dry so he was nice enough to share his drink - wouldn't drug himself right? Most of my time was spent on my back with my legs in a pretzel shape over me with him hitting it deep. It felt really good and I could feel my throat getting sore from all the moaning and screaming I had been doing in the last 24 hours. He put his full body weight on me for a long time and my legs felt like they were going to break - he's definitely not small. He licks my ass and he's actually really good at it. His tongue goes sharp and long easily and I'm thoroughly excited. I decline riding him. I play with his balls, but decline sucking and licking. Come on now, my Doctor just got it good. Although he had the most time and we played hardcore, it was getting redundant. I'm not into changing positions 50 times and holding out forever. Long story short, he shot his cum on my lips. Mmmm. Then he immediately dropped down beside me and kissed me. That was hot.

We get cleaned up, dressed and he's still messing with me a little bit here and there. We walk downstairs and I talk about a collection I found. I pick up my purse, kiss him and head for the door. He's still talking to me and I'm doing my best to answer, but I just want out. It's been more than an hour and I'm naturally freaking out. I need out. I can barely walk. My legs hurt so badly. I'm starving, so I pick up a bite to eat. I call my husband like I always do and head for home. I'm too exhausted to move, to think, and I can barely even drive. My jaws ache. My ass is in pain. I have a killer headache. I need to be home, with my family relaxing. I want a nap. I need a shower… I remember walking in the door of my house and just sitting in a recliner for hours. I was too sore to walk. My husband picked up my favorite hardy soup for me. Thank goodness! I couldn't open my mouth enough to chew if I wanted to!

CHAPTER 8

A little black book has been known for holding onto secret women in a man's life. Mine is a little different. My husband gifted this little black book to me with a dedication summarizing how he wanted me to be able to write all my escapades in it like a sexy journal. So I did... for a little while. I realized that I want to keep track of all the random, filthy, creative ideas that run through my head during the day. I can be walking through an aisle at a local big box store with a famous red circle logo and see a whisk in the kitchen section. Most people either don't pay attention to the item or decide if they need one. I however stop in mid stride, cock my head to the side on an angle, and stare at it for a solid 10 minutes. "A whisk has a good solid handle," I think to myself. "That means it would be fairly sturdy to use as a whipping tool - literally." I begin to giggle and someone walking past the aisle looks at me as if I must have just read a funny text or I'm crazy. I'm dressed professionally, so the person probably assumes I'm debating the benefits of each for cooking purposes. Oh no. The person is definitely wrong. If they only knew! My train of thought runs as follows: "Could the wire pieces hurt? Would they bruise, just leave a red line, or do nothing at all? What if I purchased the coated whisk instead of metal? Would a coated whisk be used more for effect than to inflict pain and punishment?" I'm getting wet just thinking about it. I take a quick picture of the item to remember as an item I may want to add to my play bag in the future. I send a text my husband to see if he needs me to pick up anything from the store. I run into someone from the local chamber of commerce and exchange pleasantries. Then, I'm on my way home to my family. After they've been taken care of for the evening, I sit down to email him.

"Here's an email Master… I haven't sent you one in a while and I do want you to know how much I appreciate the break you have me from typing so much. This was only a couple hours after playing, so I definitely meet the 24 hour time limit *kisses*.

I was getting stir crazy… I needed to get outta the house even just for a few minutes. I always need something from (a local big box store) and a trip to the grocery store, so I planned on running errands.

Sean and I messaged a few times about a year ago. Then I saw him again at a family holiday gathering as the boyfriend of one of my husband's cousins. After the event, I told my husband that it looked like him and he said he thought the same thing! I started weighing the pros and cons of playing with him. He's attractive. He's kinky. He's also apparently part of her life now and he wasn't when I first chatted with him. My husband breaks my train of thought and says, "Did you see him checking you out? He wanted you!" I replied, "Mmmm, I know! He couldn't keep his eyes off me! It probably didn't help that I would tease him by walking by in super tight pants showing off my voluptuous curves and sexy ass. Or I would bend over to pick up things like a dirty slut. No one else paid attention, but when I'd glance at him he looked like he may cum right then!" So, here's a story about and I planned to play yesterday, but he had to be with our family all day. I opted out of attending the party. I knew that since we weren't playing, he would be there and it would seem odd for me to all of a sudden want to spend an afternoon with all the women in his family. He messaged this morning saying how horny he was. How he wanted to fuck her and imagine his balls slapping my ass when he was hitting it. I told him to spank her like he would if he was spanking me. Apparently that made him cum hard by just thinking about fucking me while he was in her Mmmm.

You know how much I like knowing your thinking about me when you're fucking... Gah it would be so hot to hear you tell me about what you're were thinking or what happened. :)

I start driving toward the store, purchased a sweet tea, and I've been chatting a bit. I want you so bad it's like breathing. I'm near where you and I fucked the first time when I see a vehicle identical to yours. My mind is racing baby. I come back to reality and keep going.

Sean messaged asking what I was doing. I tell him I'm out running errands and my husband is home with the kids. Sean says to meet him at an old school near their house. I don't even know where this school is. I go on to the store because his wife is home, so I doubt we will meet. He sends me directions and I go see if he is going to figure out how to get away with her home within walking distance away from where we will meet."

I open kik and message you. I'll never forget you telling

me my instructions for if I meet or play. Maybe you imagine me in what I'm wearing. Maybe you like to be a little protective and know what I'm wearing just in case whoever it is kidnaps me or something. Either way, I love messaging you that I'm meeting. I get so excited messaging you - no matter if it's just to check and see how your day is or something super hot like I'm going to fuck. I have more than my usual makeup on so it's an odd coincidence he wanted to meet - mascara, eyeliner, eye shadow everything. I look hot and have very sexy eyes.

"I pull in and I don't see a car. I message that I'm at some school but I don't know if it the right one.... I drive around front and I see him walking in the parking lot. I pull up and he gets in. I ask where we can park and we drive there.

He said "we can walk around or whatever. I couldn't bring my wallet because I told her I was going out for a run and she'd wonder why I need it. We can go get condoms right up the road." I thought wow expecting huh. I stop the car and say ok we can walk around. I've never been here. He looks horny as hell and not exactly nervous just excited. We walk down and around into the middle of the outside area of this little old school. He shows me two different places he's found that look good for playing. I ask if there are cameras and there aren't.

He said, "ok let's go get condoms. You know since you want to use them." I nudge him with my arm smiling at him giving him those sexy eyes and say yeah because I want one. "Hey, you're the boss" he says. We are still walking and I give him the "whatever" phrase I typically use when I playfully brush something off. We make it toward my SUV and I said, "So what you expected me to say 'no I don't want to use one?'" He said, "no, but…" I said no but what. He's already getting in the SUV and I ask for my sunglass case. He hands it to me and says "no, but I know you so it's up to you." I said you really trust me that much. He said, "Definitely! I know how much creampies turn us both on." That's all it took! He didn't hesitate or act nervous or anything. He and his cock were past ready to fuck.

We walk back into the middle grassy area. The building surrounds us except the path we just came through. I love brick in old buildings, coffee shops, or inside a house. So, I opt to play by a brick wall. He puts his back against the wall and pulls me in close to him. We are kissing and he's good. I make him take his phone out of his pocket and put it on the grass beside mine after my hand brushes it along his side. I don't want one of us accidentally calling her!

I take the opportunity to flip him around and put my back against the brick explaining I like to be pushed up against a wall. We are kissing again. He's grabbing my boobs and moaning because he loves them. I feel how hard he is through those basketball shorts pushed against me. Mmmm gah! That's so fucking sexy.

I reach down and run my fingers across the front of his shorts. He pulls back and I want his dick down my throat. I slowly move his shorts down with one hand and have my hand around his cock with the other. He pulls them down and I'm holding him in the palm of my hand. I drop straight to my knees and start sucking him even though he's already hard. He's moaning. He face fucks me. I can tell he's getting close and I've barely been trying. She must not have a mouth like mine! I've barely been sucking a minute or two. But, I want that in my pussy. I'm not here to give a halfass blowjob and be done with it. I've wanted him for a long time and he's sure as hell going to fucking me before I leave.

He's so turned on. I'm so wet. I love sucking cock. You know how kinky it is for us to even be chatting let alone fucking because of the situation. Our spouses are cousins. We are around each other all the time. However, we can go through a get together in true Southern style without anyone having a clue we're lusting after each other. I pull off and say, "I want you to fuck me". He immediately says take your pants off. Mmmm can't wait. I stand up. Wiggle my ass out of the tight jeans because you know I never use buttons. I slide them seductively down my ass. I asked if doggy was ok and he said yes.

I bend over and put my palms flat on the ground. He sticks his dick in me and gah… I've been waiting for that. But it's not right. I want it deep and I know he won't do it deep in that position. I turn facing the wall reminding him how I like to be pushed up against a wall. I push my face up against the brick, hands on the wall like he's hitting me deep for visual effect and my ass up in the air so he can fuck my pussy well. He's about my height so I arch my back just right to fit him with my ass sticking up. He's hitting it pretty good. I'm soaking wet. It's beyond hot to be at a school. Outside. Having HIS cock buried in me. He's slowing and we all know he's about to fill me full of cum soon. It's only been a little bit of time. He's sooo turned on. He's wanted my pussy and now he's in it. He's fucking me. He asks if I want him to pull out and I say NO! He tells me he needs to slow down a bit or he's going to cum. I tell him to fuck me and give it to me. I moan really loud and he shushes me since we are outside and people are outside at their houses close by. I lower my voice a bit and keep moaning. He fucks me harder and I'm ready to take it. I feel him explode inside me and how slippery I am. I'm soaking wet! I literally butt him by pushing him outta me with a bounce of my butt. His cock is covered in cum. He looked so worried. "Do you have something in your car I can use to clean up. I didn't think about this and I can't go back like this". I mentally searched my car and only knew of my sexy fur coat. Hell no! I flashed him a sexy smile and said, "I could clean it off for you". The cocktail of my cum and his intoxicatingly mixed on him. He seemed excited, so I sucked every bit of this new cocktail off of him. I licked the base of his shaft, against his stomach, and cleaned him well before we pulled our clothes back up and walked back down the little path. He went for a run and I got back in my vehicle. I message you Daddy and call Seth. Every step I took I could feel his cum still oozing out of my pussy. It turns me on so much to know another man's cum is deep in me. I was famished so I grabbed a burger. I was so wet … My lips were sliding against each other the whole time. I needed to pee so I went and tried to take a creampie pic before while I was waiting for my food. I want my Dom. I need you to cum fuck me. Feel cum up in me. Know that your babygirl was out getting fucked on a whim but will ALWAYS come back to you. Always want you. Always need you. I'm yours and that's exactly how I like it.

I came home and wiggled my ass at Seth. I pull my jeans down my ass and say wasn't it hot knowing Sean was in me? You love knowing he filled me, don't u? He shoved his finger in my cunt and said I was soaking wet. He follows me to the bedroom and fucks me missionary and doggy. He cums and so do I. I make him finger me and lick my clit. He makes me cum and I tell him how I've had a fun day :) xoxo

CHAPTER 9

I go to work and realize I want a new job. I need a new challenge. I apply for five positions that week and get an interview for one by Friday. Within a month, I've been offered three positions and I choose the one that offers the best benefits while providing the best job duties I would enjoy. Everything seems to work right when I have my Daddy! My husband is happy. My kids are happy. I've obtained a new position. My Daddy makes me feel more confident and sexy every day! I actually run my personal business decisions by him just as I would my husband. I trust his opinion and know he wants the best for me.

Hello my sexy Daddy Dom. Here are the events of my fun weekend.

The IT guy, Engineer and Probations all are asking for more than once a month and longer than an hour. I don't have that kind of time and I'm not taking it away from my family. I've chatted with England and he's telling me how I wouldn't have any trouble at all finding men to play or men to add to my stable of penises. Hehehe. I was so sweet and innocent once.

Not anymore. Now I have a stable of men I can fuck any time I want. A cute girl with a cheek piercing messaged. She wanted to meet last night, but I was with my family. I met up with her. She had big boobs and the piercing was hot. But, she seemed to rough for my taste. I prefer the high maintenance, beautiful, professional type.

On Monday, I have a tentative play date in my hometown. I don't remember what this guy does. Chatted with him a lot in the past, never met up because he travels for work and our schedules just never matched. He's a good-looking dude, successful, and smart. We'll see how it goes.

I played with my lover! He asked for me to be in high, over-the knee boots! I made sure I was dressed exactly how he requested, very sexy and insanely tall boots that hugged every curve in my legs. That day we started experimenting with cbt. I think I found one of my new favorite things! I took the crop and tapped on his balls. Every time he jumped I felt the wicked grin on my face get wider. I kept tapping, making it a little harder each time until he looked like he was going to vomit. He didn't use his safeword, and I know he would have if it was too much, but my feelings for this man stop me from doing too much. That's something I had to work on so I could be a better Domme for him. Dominants do dominant things because they enjoy doing them, but also because the submissive actually needs those things too! I was told by a male friend of mine that is a Dom, "if you really care about him like you say you do, you'll get over the feelings of hurting him and be the Domme he needs and wants." I've never looked at it the same way since. He needs and wants it. So do I. We are a perfect match for this lifestyle. So on this day, I bring out a more dominant personality. We are at a resort today and my husband likes to golf like most men do. I stole a golf tee and golf ball out of his bag before I left. I had my submissive laying on his back propped up on pillows so he could easily see what I was doing. I was in a sexy corset with my tits about to fall out. I grab the golf accessories and lube before sitting back down on the bed. I stroke him to get him hard. I put lube all over the tip of his cock and on the golf tee. I explain since this is the first time we're trying this, he needs to be vocal about anything if it's too much. He agrees and I start slowly inserting the tee into him. I'm watching his face the entire time to make sure he's okay. He gets to one point and asks me to wait a minute. He's adjusting. He didn't say flat no to continuing or demand for me to take it out. He explores new fetishes with me and I love him for that. I continue until the tee is all the way in and I'm soaking wet! My wicked eyes light up and I'm beyond ready to go to the next step. I have the golf ball in my hand. I also brought one of the very lightweight plastic practice balls. I start with that and snap a picture. I check on him to see if he's okay and he tells me to go for the full weight of the regular golf ball. I know that will push the tee even deeper into him. I'm excited to see him attempt to take it. People do insertions so this is kind of the same thing, right? Mmmm... I place it on top and he grimaces for a minute. He's taking deep breaths then his breathing regulates. I know the look on my face is the "fuck me now" face because I'm so turned on. I take multiple pictures of him trying his Domme's new insertion fetish before I pull it out. After that, I'm ready to switch to my submissive side. Long story short, I pay for the new fetish. Please understand that we've discussed everything at length before we ever try it. I've asked for this. He pulls out rubbing alcohol, gauze, and large bandages. I know what's next before he shows me. He has a knife. He sterilizes my skin with something I didn't see from his bag because he had me up on all fours. He moves me to standing on the side of the bed and then bent over it. I'm still in the super high over the knee boots. He tells me every step of the process. He sterilizes the knife and explains that if I put rubbing alcohol I think it was on the cut every day after it, I will have the design as a scar. Fuck yeah! That's the goal! Yes, I was concerned with cutting a vein or something. But, I spoke to a doctor in the lifestyle at length before we did it! The design he picked for me was his initials. He started with one small cut and I jumped a little. He said, "baby, you have to sit still or it will mess up and I may hurt you unintentionally. Please be very still." I can feel myself shaking with excitement as adrenaline is running through me! He literally marked me! He is my owner and now my ass shows it! I had the scar for a good 3-4 months, but then it healed.

Probation and I chat and decide to meet. The morning of our play date he asks if we're still on for playing, among other things! :) I'm already swollen and excited. It's 7:30 a.m. and I already want to feel him inside me.

This is going to be a long ass day…

The longer the day goes, the more frustrated I get. I'm so impatient and I'm bored out of my mind at work although I have plenty to do. I catch myself staring at my computer screen imagining my upcoming romp. He's trouble. Ok, I have to quit thinking about it. Around 1:30 p.m. I text him "just a couple of hours and your mine." He loves feeling like I've wanted him that bad…it's so easy. I have lace panties in my pocket and every time my hand brushes by the bulge I get excited. Come on! The end of the workday cannot come fast enough!

I wasn't dressed sexy because of where I work…plus, he got sexy last time. I planned to change to lace underwear at a gas station along the way and take off my bra. I text him while I'm walking out the door from work to get an address and directions which I send to my husband. We're texting the whole way there. I stop at a gas station and the restroom is packed! There's a huge line of people coming in behind me so my plan is out the window. Grrr… I get back in the car and continue driving. He calls and I reluctantly answer. I hate talking on the phone to anyone other than my husband for any reason. To me, hearing a voice makes it more personal and there's really no reason to add that. Voices are a huge turn on for me, so I generally avoid the phone. Anyway, I answer and he asks where I am. He tells me that he could put his uniform on and I think that's hot. He says he will be dressed in his uniform and for me to undress him when I get there. Mmmm! In my book, a man in uniform is third to a man in a suit and sexy man in dark blue jeans and a black t-shirt - FYI :)

I can feel my heart racing. I can't wait to get there and get started. But, this time it's not nerves at all. I just want in the door, in his arms and on his bed. Accurate directions take me to his driveway and my phone rings as soon as I put the car in park. Oh no....it's my husband. Did my MIL flip? Do I have to stop by somewhere before I come home? Is everyone ok? He never calls me before I play and that makes me instantly nervous. I quickly answer and he's forgotten his car keys. ARE YOU SERIOUS? Long story short, after I play I'm to pick up the kids and then go pick him up at work. Great. Just Great. I get tired of the conversation and am irritated, so I walk to the front door while I'm talking to him. I walk in talking, put my stuff down and hug him. I love feeling his arms wrapped around me. I tell my husband bye and explain the situation. Dude is totally cool about it although you could see that he was disappointed. He looks good in his uniform. I say, "you put this on just for me" with a little sly smile and he said yes. I have to step up on my tiptoes so I can kiss him. He bends down and his hand is already on "the spot" on my neck. Woo Hoo... I ask to use the bathroom before we play - standard procedure - and we walk to his bedroom. He's telling me a little about his house on the way through. The doors are wide open and he's right there while I'm getting cleaned up. After all, I couldn't have him see my granny panties, now could I? :)

He has a Jacuzzi, big shower, walk in closets, and a nice size bedroom. I just have on my sweater and bra now. He gets up off his bed and walks over to me. We kiss again and he's the type that kisses a long time before he takes a breath or moves away from your face. There's definitely a place for that and it always reminds me of kissing the first guy I ever loved. They couldn't be more different otherwise. I'm kissing him and he grabs my ass. "I've missed that ass," he whispers to me. I can feel his hard cock pressed against me. Mmmm, I smile and start unbuttoning his uniform. I pull his shirt out of his pants and start on the pants. Quickly he's naked in front of me. I grab his cock and start stroking him. He tells me it's my turn and my clothes fall to the floor. I bend over and suck him. There's a lot of kissing and touching while we're walking to the bed. I sit down Indian style and suck. He told me last time I could suck him as long as I wanted to and the thought raced through my head. Oh, I want to do that. But, I have to hurry because my husband doesn't have keys.

Two seconds later, I'm on my back and he has my legs spread wide open. He licks my clit and I close my eyes. I remember this. He's good. Definitely not making a mental grocery list with this one. I'm about to cum after like 1 minute and he stops for a second. NO! He kisses and sucks the inside of my thigh then starts licking again. This time when I was close, he put a finger in me. Yes! He has big hands. It feels so good. I love it. I grab his other hand and lock our fingers. I buck up and cum on his face. I can feel it shooting out of me. He moans and is all excited. I'm sure he said something, but I don't remember. I was enjoying the "after" as he was kissing my thigh. I didn't get 2 minutes before he was at it again. Two fingers and a talented tongue take me to #2. He doesn't stop there and there's a 3rd before he even moves. He comes up and sucks on my nipple. I pull his face up and kiss him hard. I taste myself all over him. I love kissing a man after he's licked me so well. I love the weight of a man on top of me, pressing into me. I lock my legs around him and start rocking him myself. We're kissing and he's pulling my hair. He pulls my head back even farther on the bed and goes for my neck. It doesn't tickle like normal... I just can't handle it, so I stop him. He says, "I think you're wanting something" and I agree.

He reaches over me and grabs a condom. I feel him sink deep and I'm smiling. His cock feels so good. He leans over me and I really like feeling a man on top of me. Yes! He's hitting it hard and talking the whole time. My orgasm overwhelms me as I cum hard on him. He kisses me and keeps on thrusting. I think he was on every angle and my head was hanging off the side of the bed. I hate that and usually can't even enjoy myself if that happens. But, that is not what would happen this time. I tell him how much I love his cock before I even realize I'm saying it. The last time he was up and over me using that curve just right. He pulled my head up and cradled it against his forehead where I couldn't move unless it was to kiss him - Omg - it was so good! I suck on his pussy-covered fingers while he's hitting it hard and I feel the rush go all over me :)

I ask him what he wants and he says me riding him. I whine no. He smiles and says yes. We go round and round a couple times. Two seconds later he's perpendicular to me in his back pulling on me. I pull back and whine a little more forcefully that I don't want to. Dude pulls me from my back to laying on top of him then sitting on him. He literally leaves no option for NO. I start riding him and he said to ride it hard because he can tell I'm just trying to control the situation. Whining didn't work, so I probably shouldn't even try that one anymore with him. I gave in to ride him how I like it. I'm riding hard and fast. It's super deep and I cum quickly riding anyway. I know the curve will get me even faster. He grabs my hips and rocks me back and forth so hard things are falling off his headboard. I feel myself slipping into another zone. I can't think at all and I am totally, completely enjoying the moment. Nothing else matters and I'm getting it good. After I cum, I lean down and kiss him.

I'm more than satisfied and ask how he wants it. He said more riding with his silly grin. I said no. He grabbed my hips and made me start riding him again. You'd think I would have learned by now… I rode him harder than I think I normally ride my husband - maybe the hardest ever. I came hard and I was moaning deep. I can see that look come over his face and he tells me he's about to cum. He says he wants to fill me up and that actually throws me off for a minute although I don't show it. It makes me think, but he starts rocking me faster and pulls me out of my thoughts. I love watching a guy's face when he cums. He stiffens his whole body and I could barely move on him. He came a lot and I try to jump off. He has my legs locked under his - now I regret telling him that's how I like to ride - and he wouldn't let me off. I kiss him, he lets me off, and he lies there like he wants to rest. I pull him up and then I lay there because I worked hard damn it. I see his tattoo for the first time. I love tattoos. He comes back to the bed and fingers me to cum again! He's trouble…

We hurried to get dressed; he's in the bathroom with me and tells me how his counters are high - perfect for fucking me on them. I say maybe next time. He's back beside me kissing and playing with my ass. Why do I have to leave again? Oh yeah… I sit on the bed to put my socks on. He comes back and teases me by telling me about his comfortable Tempurpedic pillows. I tell him to quit because I of course want to lie there with him for a few minutes then play again, but I can't.

I snuggle up in the crook of his arm, kiss him hard and tell him to quit teasing me. I lie there a second. Little things catch my attention… Someone's voice. The way they smell before and after sex… He says he's still hard if I want to go again and puts my hand on his cock. I start rubbing it. No, no, no! I must go, but damn I want it. Wtf? Why couldn't he remember his keys?! I put my necklace on and he helps me by pulling my hair out from under the chain. He pressed up against the back of me and grabs my boobs. Then, he grabs my hips. I push him away. I don't get far because in no time he's back behind me. This time he gently moves the hair on the side of my neck and starts kissing. I can feel myself start melting into him and I'm pushing my ass into him.

I grab his hand and pull him out of his room because I know I'll never get outta that house.

He took me on a tour of his place. I saw a couple of pictures on the fireplace mantle of his extended family. Nice kitchen and he explained how he cooks…love that. He's handy at fixing things up around the house. All of which are hot. We get back to the door and I'm on my tiptoes having to kiss him. He's grabbing my ass. I knew he was going to do it and I didn't even have time to say no. He picks me up and wraps my legs around him. My boobs are burying his face and I'm so fucking turned on I couldn't care less how Seth gets home. I straighten my legs and whine to get down. He puts me down and I kiss him. We say our goodbyes and I leave with an open invitation to come back whenever I want. He said if I wanted to fuck early in the mornings before work, he'll be there waiting for me naked. Mmmm! So tempting!

I text him that I hate I had to hurry so much. I know I'll have to make it up to him and I may have to pay up in a couple of days. Whenever he says, I'm there.

I had the chance to meet up with my Dom today! He asked that I wear a corset and sexy heels. Yes Sir! I go to the room and put on a leopard corset, black booty panties and heels. I throw on my hair is down and I look like a dominatrix. I have a crop in my hand when I let him in. He kisses me and we get started. Today is picture day! I love pictures. The more original the layout and subject of a photograph, the more excited I am. We found a few pictures online and I knew what we had planned for the day. I stand on the bed, yes in high heels, while he's lying naked on his back. He's propped up on pillows under his neck. I place my right foot onto his chest. He's moaning and rubbing my leg, obviously turned on by the sight of my sexy tan, smooth legs. I apply a little body weight to the right leg and I hear him go through the varying levels of discomfort. The heel of my shoe is digging into his chest. He thought this would be a good picture. I was okay with doing it, but not so overly excited about it. I did the routine of standing on him a few times and then I saw it. My submissive had a few red circles on him, looking as if he had been burned with a cigarette. As it turns out, he was right! That was extremely hot and made for a very sexy photo! He was hard the whole time. I wonder how he hid that from her? Hehehehe.

Next up that day was the photo I requested, a pistol. I know that may sound completely insane, but I trust this man! I brought my own handgun and he brought his as well. I had found a photo online of a man with one hand on a girl's neck and the other holding a pistol with the tip in her mouth. Maybe edge play isn't your thing, but OMG I definitely have this side to me! I had the sexy leopard corset on, my head on the corner of the bed and my hair falling off over the side. He had one palm against my throat gripping tight while the other held the pistol in my mouth. Yes, don't try this at home and I'm not condoning this for everyone. We both checked each gun multiple times to make sure they were not loaded! My gun is powerful, but his is more powerful and definitely looked better in the photo. We played hard after that and I left tasting gun oil in my mouth for the rest of the evening!

CHAPTER 10

Ok… I think this is everything…

I had to cut the session short last time and I said I'd make it up to him. It looked like I may be able to pay up two evenings from then, but nothing was set in stone.

I had been gone for a few hours shopping, meeting, visiting with my family, etc. I get home and bring in my purchases. Tell my husband hi and that I love him. Kiddos are happy to see me and I was ready to play with them. Literally 10 minutes after I'd been in the house, I got a message saying his parents just left and he's free. I debate going back out for about 15 minutes. I leave the decision up to my husband. He says to go. I take off the button up, keep on the navy camisole with lace across the top and throw on a hoodie. I kiss him goodbye, give big hugs to the kids and I'm out the door. I feel like a bad mom. I know everyone has hobbies and there's nothing wrong with that, but women are made to feel like they are suppose to be with the kids all the time and definitely more than the men. I click out of my mood and into playing. My husband wants me to go. He wants me to have fun. I message you Daddy as soon as I get in the car in my driveway so that I don't forget one of your rules...

I text saying I'll be there soon and then again right before I get there. I switch out of my Clark boots and put on my high-heeled snakeskin boots. I walk up the steps to the deck and straight up to the door. The door was open and I walk on in like I've been there a million times. I open the door and ask if I need to knock or if I can just come on in. He gets up out of the chair he's sitting in walks over to me and wraps his arms around me while planting a huge kiss on me. With the high heels on I can reach his face much better. He stops long enough to ask me how long we have this time and I ask him how long he wants. He said, "I don't know, but I'm sure you have to go home sometime." Haha. Umm...yeah. I say yes, but I have a little while. We kiss again and he starts to lead me to his room. I stop him so that I can sit on the couch in the front room and take my boots off. No tour this time. He takes my hand and we start walking with me in front to his room. Kissing again, he bends down really far because he's so tall! He's kissing my neck. His hands are all over me. I flip around to face him and am immediately engulfed in his arms. I'm told to get on the bed and I have to suck again for a few minutes. It's so nice! He tells me to lay back and he climbs up over me. I love the weight of a man! He's kissing me passionately. I can't catch my breath. He has his fingers in my hair and pulls my hair just a little causing my head to tilt to the side so that he can kiss my neck. I pull away, but he goes right back. I start rocking him with my legs and he stops. He looks at me and says "I think someone wants that in them" and of course I do. Within minutes he's grabbing his first condom. He sits up and places it down his shaft. Then he's laying on me again. He wasn't super rough, but definitely made his point by sinking it in deep the first time. I gasp and he smiles. I get slow easy lunges for a little while so that I can get use to it.

That curve…! No joke I literally cum about every 2 minutes with this dude. There's no reason to even try to keep track… He sucks on my nipples and I wrap my legs tight around his waist. He hits it deep over and over… I can't even stop myself from cumming. I finally catch hold of my thoughts and stop him. I tell him I want to ride him and he smiles so big. He's flat on his back and I'm quickly over top of him. He guides his cock in me and I start slowly. He tells me to go as fast as I can and I say no. He just does it because he knows I'll say no and he will get his way. I tell him one day I'll quit saying no and that he'll have me trained. He holds my hips and hits deep within my throbbing, hot, wet walls himself. The curve is just a touch painful because it's so deep with me riding him. It fills me full. After cumming twice, he grabs hold of me tight and tells me he's about to cum. I watch his body as it goes through his orgasm. It's such an exciting thing to watch.

We're both hot and sweaty. He asks if I need anything to drink and I say I'm good. He said he had to have something so he offers again. He says he has freshly brewed sweet tea he made himself. We walk naked to the kitchen and he pours me some tea. While he's getting glasses and other items needed, he takes little moments to swat my ass when he walks by. He's showing me different photos and things before we head over to his living room couch. This is already too "comfortable" for me, but I'm trying to get through it without thinking. We sit there watching the History channel and he has his arm wrapped around me like we're in high school or something. He runs his fingers across my arm. He plays with a nipple. I turn around to kiss him. That was actually nice. He starts rubbing on me and I wrap his arms around the top of my chest. I kiss his arms and bite just a little here and there. He warned me that if I started he would finish. Ok, enough said. He reached down toward my pussy and I grabbed his hand. There's really no reason because he's so strong. He says to sit still and I protest. Finally he convinces me and he lightly plays with my clit. It's like magic because I'm automatically excited. I arch my back into him and put my head on his shoulder. His arm right arm is over my chest and I'm gripping it with both hands because it's so intense. He had been telling me about how he likes to give massages and I'm a sucker for a good massage. After his playing he tells me to get up and follow him because it's time for my massage. He takes my hand and leads me to the bedroom. He has me walk in first and tells me to lie down. I lay on my stomach because nothing relaxes me more than someone rubbing my back…like ever since I was a baby. I'm not sure if I'll be able to play again after this…

He grabs his stuff and straddles me with his cock resting on my ass. Tease. I hate lubes, oils, new soaps, or anything that I could potentially be allergic to by using. Fine. I'm just going to chill and go with it. I hear him click the top of the bottle open and then feel the swirls he creates on my back with it. His hands are exactly like I said I wanted it… deep, but not painful. My lower back, my shoulders, long strokes and small deep circles…it all feels wonderful. I could seriously fall asleep if he did it too long. I tell him how good it feels. He's telling me how he's spoiling me and massages are part of what a good boy toy does. Mmmm… He mentions how he is on a better angle to smack my ass and I get one quick smack.

In no time I'm back under him, but not for long. He kisses the side of my neck and I feel them rush down me. The chill bumps…No…. He can't learn that too. I use every bit of force to push him off me and he's surprised that I could push on him so hard. He looks at me funny with a surprise on his face. He smiles saying, "Wow." He's had his hand at the spot the whole time and the mix of the two was a little much. He never has to hit it hard since I cum so fast with him in me. Each time he gives me a few seconds before starting again. He's always over me, then higher, then completely over top of me with my head hanging off the bed. Finally he asks what I want and I tell him I want to ride him. There's that smile again…he knows he's won. He teases me asking if I really want to and I start begging just a little. He comes off and I hop on. I ride him like there's no tomorrow! After I finished riding the wave of my second orgasm, I jump off and tell him I want him behind me. I'm on my knees and his bed has a wooden headboard with shelves on each side. I'm looking straight into a mirror when he deep into me. I see myself wince. Maybe the curve isn't the best for the doggie position. He's big. It's painful. I like it deep, hard, and rough. But, this is enough to make me scream louder than normal. I'm grabbing the base of the headboard in front of me. I see the pain on my face and just put my head down. We always talk dirty during sex and that keeps it super fun. I finally can't take it any deeper. I tell him I want him back over me. I know I've had twenty orgasms since we started playing today, but I'm sure it's more. The number continues to climb and there's so much pressure on my head. I can't hear anymore, so I tell him I'm done. I feel bad because he didn't cum a second time before I was done. How many times are we going to go? I know he said it takes him forever to cum the second time, but I don't have forever. I lay there with his arms around me. We kiss every once in a while. I flip to my stomach while we attempt to figure out how many times I came. I tell him I never bother to count with him and remind him that he didn't even spank me. I'm lying on my side and have pinned his left arm under me. He reaches up and smacks my ass hard. "Woo!" After about 8 or 9 more of those, my ass is on fire. I tell him that I hate to go, but I really must. We get up and he laughs. He says, "You should see how red your ass is." I tell him it would make it hurt more if I saw. Again, maybe I'll learn. He takes me in the bathroom, spins me around, and tells me to look. OMG!

He laughs and says that was just his left hand and that I wouldn't allow him get a good smack at it even with his left. I can't imagine what his right can do! He disposes of the condom and says that I can just take a shower there. I decline because I know he's trying to get me to shower with him and his two showerheads. I usually don't clean up after and go straight home to my husband. That's how this works. I'm back in the room getting my stuff together. I put my bra on and he grabs my nipple. I try to be cute and playful. I stop his hand from going between my legs. He's lying on the bed watching me dress. He tells me to wait and then he disappears into the kitchen. He comes back with ice for my ass. He tells me to turn around and he rubs the ice on each cheek. The second it touches my ass the ice is completely melted. He's amazed at how hot my ass is and how fast the ice melts. I pull my black lace panties on and even the lace is painful. The jeans weren't much better. I can feel the heat radiate off my ass! He's back to the sexy gentleman by kissing and rubbing. He's grabbing but not like I'm a piece of meat. He's grabbing like he's savoring every inch of me. He offers to get me an ice pack to use for my ass on the way home and I decline. I lead him out and he asks if I want any tea to take with me. See, it's the little things that matter to me. I say yes and he pours some while I head to my purse. I did take my little whip, but he only used it once and it wasn't very hard. He remembered that he had it and went and got it for me before I left. I grab my phone and notice a message from you :) I tell you that I'm leaving while I'm standing in his kitchen. I'm smiling when he comes back with the whip because now I'm thinking about playing with you. The whip reminded me of you Samson. My playmate threatened to go buy me a toy and make me use it if I didn't bring one next time... I totally believe him.

I go back to grab my purse and walk out the door after kissing him and saying goodbye, not even bothering to put my boots back on. I just got it so good that I'm not 100% sure about walking in little high-heeled boots. I message my husband when I get in the car. OH! It hurts to sit! It hurts to laugh. It hurts to cough. It just hurts. I'm going to be sore for a couple of days. He is going to meet me in another town so that I won't have to drive all the way home myself. Super nice. I'm chatting with you, my husband, and the Probationer on the way to meet up. I tell my husband the story all the way home. When I get in the door of my house, I message him to let him know I got home safely. He can't have his fuck buddy getting hurt I guess. When we get home we feel the ridges on my ass from his fingers when he smacked it. My husband washes the massage oil off my back. It's sexy to have a husband who will love you and enjoy the lifestyle with you.

The next day he asks if I'm sore, how much I enjoyed him, and when I'm coming back. I say tomorrow and he said he's free tomorrow morning, off Wednesday, and Thursday. I say that's a little soon don't you think and that I'll be sore for a day or two. He loves it. My husband informed me I was actually playing for an hour and 45 minutes last time. Yep, I knew I'd hear that one... But, in all fairness, I only had like 30 minutes last time. So, I'm only 15 minutes over between two sessions :)

CHAPTER 11

I'm planning all of the last minute items I need to buy for Christmas presents. I've finished decorating the house with Christmas trees, garland, and lots of lights! My family enjoys the holidays!

I get up, grab my phone, and turn my music on. I start a hot shower. It's the same routine. Every day. I go look for lace panties and jump in the shower. I like to take a shower with water as hot as I can get it. I took the extra time to shave well for him. I'm already extremely wet just going through the motions of getting ready for the playdate. It's such a turn on.... I get dressed, say bye, and message the engineer. I stop to grab a sweet tea because I'd be late anyway. I tell the engineer he can call and I talk to him for 15 minutes or so on my way. The end of a shower on his end of the call stopped that conversation flat - but the risk was TOTALLY hot. I was so ready to play after that conversation... And, I was flying down the highway to get there to relieve the tension.

He messages me and says, "Come on in when you get here." Ok, that's new. I say,"Yes sir." That was the entire conversation until I walked in their door, down the hallway and into the room. I place my sunglasses down on their table and climb on the bed toward him. He's laid out on his side wearing only tight boxer shorts. I kiss him and he's really into it. As in he's OVERLY into it. But, something's different. Who cares, that's how I like it! :) He flips me to my back and doesn't stop kissing. He slides my shirt up and yanks my bra down to suck and bite my nipple. Before I know it, he's kissing my lips, neck, and then painful bites to my neck. Ouch! Did I walk in the wrong place? I'm moaning and rubbing the back of his head. He pulls me on top of him, but my long cowl neck sweater is getting in the way. I yank it off along with the cute long silver necklace I'm wearing. I throw everything across the room. He unhooks my bra and grabs my boobs tight. Moaning. Kissing. Grabbing. Mmm…. I've never allowed myself ride him, but at that moment I wanted it. He has his hands in my jeans yanking on them and then my panties. He slides down under me and bites my pussy through my jeans. I swear I thought he tore a hole in the crotch and I knew I was going to see my family after, but I didn't care. It was just like being eaten.

He pushes me forward, jumps up, and pulls the jeans and panties down to my knees. He's yanking my shoes and socks off and I hear the shoes hit the hardwood floor. He pushes me again and clothes are completely off in seconds. I'm up on my knees and he's under me eating me. That's another thing I haven't done with him. His tongue is magic! I cum on his face in seconds! His tan, toned body pushed up against the back of me. He's really into it and I feel him poke the tip of his cock at the entrance to my pussy. When it comes down to it, I just want it. Hard. Fast. Deep. For a while just like that... I'm getting tipped and when I look around at him I see that look on his face. He starts hitting it hard. He still has his boxers on and the material isn't soft by any means. He usually does one position for just a little bit before changing. Not this one. It was rough - literally - and I could feel my pussy getting irritated from the fabric, but I was so excited by it too. He pulled my hair hard. I came on him and I loved seeing his big rock hard cock with a huge wet place on his boxers all down the shaft. He was immediately under me eating me again. I arch my back and he wraps his legs around the top of me. Then, I lean back with my hands on his thighs. I grab his cock and I'm happy to feel he's still hard. I cum two more times before he placed me on my back.

He tips it in for a while and he has that serious look in his eyes. I don't understand. If he's willing to do that, what's the difference in that and hitting me bareback and pulling out? He's fixed…. I don't get it. He had condoms by his pillow this time. I couldn't take it too long before I wanted it. He put one on and did his rough sideways back and forth motion that makes me cum quickly. We go to missionary, then scissoring. It's not my favorite position, but it feels okay. I finally get up on my knees and he slides it in really easy, then back out. That was all he did for a minute. Next thing I know he rams it in me hard. I scream in surprise before getting a series of 10 more times just like that. It was so hard and painful, but fun! I know he can't be on his knees much, so I'm surprised he did all of that. He turned me back on my back, kissing me, biting my lip, and sinking it deep. I had little time to think. But, I'll admit, the engineer told me to think of my Dom while we were playing and I did. I was thinking about what he'd be saying if I was playing with him. He seems like he would be so good at talking during play, says he enjoys it, and by that point I'm distracted. I have to look away just to make sure I don't lose focus on actually playing in the moment. I keep thinking, "Talk Damn It!" But, nothing. Not for long. He jumps off the bed, taps the cover and yanks my ass over the edge of the bed. He makes me come again, but I'm not done.

He starts to get off the bed and I said, "lie down." Doing as he's told, he just looks at me. I tell him how I want to ride him while I'm grabbing his cock tight and shoving it in my pussy. I lower down on it slowly to feel every inch and tell him to lock my legs under him. I'm riding him and he's more excited than I've ever seen him. He has his hands over his head hanging off the bed, so I grab them. I tell him to put them behind his head and hold his hands firmly in place against the bed. I sit back and ride it pretty well, but not as hard as I do the probationer or my husband. I cum all over him and he's so turned on. Just as I was about to come down from my orgasm, he tightens his grip on my hands and starts bouncing me more than he had been with his hips. I know there were a few times I was completely airborne! Fuck it was hot! He was 100% serious and it's exciting to see a guy take what he wants. That's definitely what he was doing. I came again! Screaming hard the whole time, I watched his face as he came with me bouncing on his cock. He was beyond excited, so I leaned down just to kiss his lips once and got off.

My husband has been sick the last few days, so I skipped the play date that day. I'm very glad he's feeling better and the rest of us didn't get it! It's only a few days until Christmas! The next morning would be early - up at 5:30 - just to play. It's amazing what I'll do to play!

I pull up a little late and he's still in uniform. He already texted to say he'd leave it on for me. He greets me at the door with a kiss causing me to stand on my tiptoes. He shows me how he's rearranged his living room while his arms wrapped tight around me. I love being in a man's arms. Mmmm, there's nothing like it. I take him by the hand and lead him to his room. He tells me to explain about the swing he'll be fucking me in. I tell him a little, but mainly just tease him.

I grab for his belt. He pulls his shirt off and then all of his clothes are off and scattered in the floor. I pull my jeans off while he's getting condoms ready. He sits down and we start kissing. He's a passionate, forceful kisser. I push him onto the bed and climb on top of him. We kiss and then all my clothes were thrown onto the floor on top of his. He wanted to tease me with the tip of his cock on my clit. Playfully, I declined by pulling it away and saying, "no, no, no."He didn't seem too pleased, but got over it quickly.

He's so tall. Samson, it's your fault you know. Tall wasn't even on the list and was actually something I didn't like until you. But now, tall is a prerequisite.

He's upright over me before pressing his full body weight into me. He's a strong dude, so there's a lot of pressure. I wrap my legs tight around him and thrust his body upward closer to me. I pushed him in and out of me until I couldn't take it anymore. I want it. Why are we wasting time? This is why he likes two+ hours. Come on dude! We can do touchy feely after the first round. Let's go already!

Is he confident or cocky? I'd say both actually. He leaned over to pick one up and before he even opened it he said, "you're going to cum the minute I put it in you." Cocky. We both know he's right. Three thrusts -

that's all it took. He smiles and it's painful. It had been a couple of weeks, so he was stretching my pussy out again. He told me a night or two before that I would have to count how many times I came the next time we played. I lost count at 10 because I wanted to enjoy it. Approximately 90% of the time, he's over me in different angles with my legs on his shoulders with my feet occasionally wrapped around his neck. That's how I like it and I usually redirect play that way if it looks like he's going to do anything else.

He's hitting it hard. It's always hard. He hit is so hard my neck is sore today. I'm always surprised I can breathe after playing with him. He wanted me to ride him and there's no reason to attempt to say no. He gets what he wants or takes it if I refuse. I jump on him and ride. Omg it feels so good. That curve is amazing and takes me into a different zone altogether. After I came the first time he made me ride him harder. I was so wet that I couldn't get any traction. I was still able to cum. I made him let go of my wrists and legs since he was holding me on him.

He's back on top of me. He has stamina and energy like I've never seen. He fucks me on every angle just long enough to tease me before switching to the next one. He's sweating on me and that's such a turn on! Trust me, I'm too much of a princess to enjoy a sweaty man. So being turned on by it takes me by surprise.

He tells me to ride him. He wants me to rock on him with my feet flat on the bed. I say no adamantly and he tries to pull my feet out from under his legs. I wiggle away, but he eventually gets his way. He knows what I knew all along. I knew it would be painful to ride him that way, so I was trying to prevent the pain. He's so big. It's so deep. I do as he asks and immediately feel it. OMG!!!! Stretched. Pain. Pleasure. He puts one hand on my shoulder to hold me down and one on my hip. He rocks me himself. HARD! I'm bruised a little from his grip in both places. I couldn't stop him if I wanted to. He's so much stronger than I am. I've never cum so hard in my entire life. I couldn't think straight at all and I loved every second of it.

He's back on top of me, and then I pull his condom off, spit in my hand and clean him off. I suck him for about 10 minutes. He's constantly rock hard.

We lie there on his bed cuddling. He likes the touchy feely stuff. For some reason, it turns him on. He's caressing me. We are kissing and he locks my head down so I can't move. I was rarely even getting to breathe.

He's more excited now. He has chill bumps running up my arms and I'm soaking wet. My head goes off the bed for the second time and I almost fall off. I told him I want him to cum on my boobs. He said I'd have to be ready because he's quick when he cums. I'm lying on my stomach and he's rubbing my ass. He said to stay just like that. He grabs his lube and shoves his cock in me. He had my legs super tight together, using me to jack his cock off.

He tells me to get on my knees. Yes sir. Awfully demanding. It's cute watching him try to Dom. He shoved it in and I gasped. The curve isn't the best for doggie. It's so big that it's painful. He said, "yeah, but you like pain." Damn it… He's right ;). He took it easy on me for a few thrusts, then I shoved my ass back to sink it in me. He picked up his pace and it hurt! I love the pain! He warned me to be ready. I told him to cover my back and that I liked to be a good little cum slut. It's like magic - he immediately pulled out and whipped the condom off. The rewarding heat from his cum shot all over my ass and dropped down my pussy. Fuck that was good!

He played for an hour and a half straight. After I cleaned off with a towel, we laid there. I was in his arms cuddling, chatting, and kissing. I had 7 minutes left to get up, shower, and out the door. It wasn't going to happen. He goes to get me a towel for the shower and I hop in. He's talking to me the whole time. I get dressed, kiss him, and go to the door. More touching and kissing then quickly out the door. That's it. I'm not as sore as I normally am a few days after. My husband said that he could definitely tell I had been with him. After a few lines of chatting, we're both ready to play again tonight. But, I'm baking like a good wife and mother!

CHAPTER 12

I was 23 minutes late. I left late and we had to pick up our other vehicle. I was chatting with T all the way down there. MMMM…that curve. T had me all worked up and ready to go before I even arrived. The month rule is going to have to go - I just can't keep myself away from that one that long. I might have to take him up on this week… Gosh, that's soon! Can I really do once or twice a week? OMG! I don't know, maybe we should play once every two weeks. I'm so glad I took a chance on that one.

I pull in and walk to the door. We're walking to the room and he said he has a surprise for me. The construction guy is hot, tan, and completely hairless. OMG I could play with him for days! I kiss him and I feel my face light up. Doesn't really matter what the surprise is, all that matters to me is that he put effort and thought into it. He's smiling and lets me walk in first. I see the swing hanging over the bed and I'm beaming. I'd asked for it and suggested it a few times before, but I had no idea I would get to try it out! I hadn't tried a swing before, but always wanted one myself. Of course, my husband had vetoed such a purchase. When I saw the hook above this man's bed the first time, I was instantly excited. Although I'm excited, I'm always nervous trying new things. I'm on the bed and we're on our knees kissing while we undress each other. He sees me second guess sitting in the swing, so he says, "just trust me." That's all it took. I've always trusted him. He's so down to earth and laid back. I sit down and he places the strap on my back and places my feet up in the stirrups. *Side Note: I hate feet. I hate people touching my feet. I hate being near anyone else's feet. I don't mind someone rubbing my legs with their feet or vice versa, but seeing or feeling hands or mouths on anyone's feet freaks me out.

He spreads my legs wide open and starts licking. Gah! He's so good. I've missed that. I really do need to take lessons from him! It's so hard to even think about what to say when he's doing that to me. And, he isn't much of a talker anyway. I really like talking! He knows exactly how to get me to cum all over his face. Five minutes after getting in the swing, my head is tilted completely back, the swing is moving, he's eating me good, and my feet are enjoying the resistance from the straps. I flip my head up quickly after the first wave and feel the blood rush. Woo!

He bites the inside of my thighs, not lightly, but definitely not hard enough to leave bruises. After 5 bites, he buries his face in me again. I'm so sensitive and I absolutely love his tongue. He's rubbing my back and pulling me toward his face. He lightly runs his fingertips across my ass, which makes me giggle. Three minutes later and I'm cumming again. I'm grabbing his head and he doesn't stop. It's nice being able to be loud. This guy never really gives me a break between orgasms long enough to gather my thoughts. He pulled his face back and I wondered what was next. I thought maybe I would get to suck him earlier than normal and maybe longer :) No. He pushes the swing back from him and I'm looking right at him. I don't usually do that for very long while I'm actually playing. Every time the swing got close to his face, he would lick me. Wow, that was hot! It felt good. Then after a few more licks, I wanted him to make me cum. I knew I wanted to beg for it, but we're just not like that. Around 10 licks, I began growing more frustrated with every lick. He finally quit rubbing my back as I swung toward and away from him. He grabbed me and went at it. My feet were pushing on the base of the loops that keep me from getting free. He pulls me closer to his face and I arch my back. I'm completely lost in the bliss.

He smiles and stands up. I suck him and it never takes long for him to get hard and close. I really enjoy giving oral. I could do it all day. He's obviously having fun and I'm ready. We play and I have a good time. When it's time for me to go, I get dressed and he walks me to his door. A sexy kiss is exchanged and I'm on my way to go shopping!

Disclaimer: I'm learning that part of my position with you is to be completely honest. I'm doing my best. I'm telling you things whether I think it's something that will make you think, take offense or find totally hot.

There's no one I'd rather have there than you. Husband included. We both know how that would have gone, so I'll save space in the email and leave that out. Again truth - I want it. I'm forward and you like that. But, I respect you too much to push anything - although believe me if I could :)

We chat later when we get home. A couple I've been chatting with for my husband and I got all interested in him after hearing how much I like him. They ask for his screen name and you know me... I don't give out people. I tell them I'll contact him and let him contact them if he's interested...which I'm sure he will be since I was. They ended up wanting him and me at a place they have on some lake an hour or two away. Hmm. I don't know. He already offered on the way down for me to be his playdate at a swinger's club party coming up even though he knows I don't do that and that's why he hasn't asked before. The guy from the couple asks a lot of questions and they're just trying to get started playing. After chatting with the probationer he's stepped up his conversation a little bit and says I'm the girl every guy dreams of having...how funny. What a line dude! All I can think is how different you and I are than he and I are. If he thinks I'm every guy's dream, I wonder what you think? Hehe.

CHAPTER 13

I work hard every day. I try to teach my children things that will make them more intelligent and cultured. I like being eclectic and definitely not boring. I'm working on a project at work that could land me a promotion if I do it well. It's time for a change and I need to make it happen. I'm a young, sexy professional. If I want something, I'm going to make it happen! I run into someone I know at work. The person ends up asking me about an item I wear showing my Dom owns me, much like a husband owns a wife with a wedding ring. I've never been able to lie to this person, so I message my Dom. I don't know what to do. My Dom asks me if I'm ashamed of him. Are you kidding me? Not at all baby. Quite the opposite! So, the guy ends up getting an education on terms such as dominant, submissive, ownership, etc. It's a whole new world he didn't even know existed. Shortly after that, we met at an area park. We kissed a little and left. We texted frequently and I learned he had never played with anyone since he married his wife. I also learn he was in a fraternity in college. What? The sweet, innocent one was in a frat?

And, he played around before he got married, so as it turns out, he definitely wasn't boring. The next time we met, it was in the parking lot of a major store in our area. We climbed in the back and fucked until he filled me full. This man knows my entire family and could ruin my life if he ever told. But, why would he? Having sex with me is too good to risk losing it if he told anyone!

Remember Sean? He's the guy dating my husband's cousin. Long story short, my husband wasn't comfortable with Sean and I playing. He said he just knew this guy would end up marrying his cousin because it would make it so hard for us. And, he was right! They did get married! Sean tried to fuck me on his wedding day and even asked right in front of our family. If there's someone that likes to play with fire, it's this guy! We've fucked at his house in their bed. He's more sweet and easy, almost making love when we are at their house. I doubt he intends to be like that, but he is. We've played in hotel rooms multiple times. We've fucked in parks. We've fucked in very busy shopping mall parking lots in the daytime with tons of cars passing by us. We both enjoyed having sex in front of so many people, knowing they could bust us at any moment. We also loved that we were having sex in the back of her vehicle while she was at home. He sends me sexy messages and photos. I do the same back with him. And when we are around each other at family functions, the stare between us makes me so wet and needy for cock! I know he's dying to be inside me and that has to do until we can sneak off to play.

One of my favorite stories is when we were at a family Christmas event. The person's house is full of family members, approximately 50 people. I walk in with him and his in laws. He opens the door to allow them to go in first. They thank him, obviously because they think he's such a considerate man. My ass! He just wanted to hold the door open and get them inside so that he could follow me in. I gave him a devilish grin and he winked at me. Anyone could have seen this. Then, he starts rubbing on my ass and spanked me! Right there inside the front door with about 15 people right in front of us. It was his turn for the evil grin before we went our separate ways. I knew that if I had felt the front of his khakis, I would have grabbed on to a raging hardon. We go through the event. I am friendly, but focused on my family. He and I exchange "I want to fuck you now stares" every once in a while. I see him gesture to go outside. He finds a reason to walk by me and then stand behind me. He says, "In just a few minutes when I signal you, let's meet outside and fuck." I told him that they would see us both leave, but he didn't care. He had to be inside me right then. And, I'm a cumslut that loves playing with him. I say ok and look at my husband sitting a few people away. He has this look on his face that tells me he definitely doesn't want Sean and I to play. I'm headstrong and I'm a HotWife. When I want to fuck, I fuck. I made a kissy face at my husband Seth so that he understood it's going to happen. He shook his head and no one has any idea of the conversation the three of us have just had. I feel my pussy get hot and start swelling. I need him. I glance over at him and he looks like he's going to cum with anticipation. About 10 minutes later he gives a signal and my heart begins to race. I wait 2 minutes and then join him outside. We find a dark secluded area behind a vehicle to hide us away from anyone that may pop out for some reason. He hikes up my dress and tells me to spread my legs. He has the most amazing view of my ass, sexy boots, and I'm bent over holding on to the vehicle waiting for him to enter me. "Mmmm fuck baby. I've wanted this all night. Have you? You're such a dirty girl." I'm moaning with every thrust, trying not to be too loud. I say, "yes, I am a dirty girl and I've been wanting you in me since you smacked my ass." After a few minutes of hot primal sex, I put my hand over my mouth to muffle my screams of passion while he explodes inside me. It feels so naughty to be right there with everyone while I'm getting my pussy filled with cum. I pull my panties back up and my dress down while he zips his pants up. I turn around and we kiss for a while before we see someone come outside. Shit! I knew it! My husband is in a hurry and speaking very loudly. He is speaking to someone saying how he or she has a lot of stuff to carry out. Oh thank god for a good husband! He's signaling us that other people are coming outside. Right behind him was a nosey family member. Shew. He saved us. Sean rushes in the house and I stay to walk back in with my husband. Merry Christmas to us!

That weekend my husband and I decide to go to a swinger's club. I message my Daddy Dom. We sign up to attend a party in the State Capital. It looks like a huge party building and a ton of attractive people have signed up. We chatted with a few couples, played pool, flirted some, touched some, but didn't play for a few hours. One man from the couples we were hanging out with was too pushy. So we go to the next place. I read about it on the Internet, saw pics, etc. But, I still wasn't 100% sure what to expect. It's a dungeon with private membership only. I'm surprised I even got him in the door. I make him walk through first. Someone comes to greet us and sign us up. I had emailed the owner back and forth for the last few weeks and he will be sponsoring us! We walk in the gallery and I don't even want to look at my man. I know it's like culture shock and I don't want to influence his initial opinion and reaction. We end up being there close to two hours, just watching of course. He's not going to do any of those things to me, but it was SOOOO easy to imagine you there, Sir! I crave you here with me. I crave you restraining me to the St. Andrew's Cross. I crave you flogging me. I crave you ordering me to lie across the spanking bench, so that you can spank me hard with whatever paddle you brought. I saw so many subs on the spanking bench. I saw a Dominatrix wear the fuck out of a man's ass with a paddle. She had to grab the medical kit. I knew from where I was sitting that she had busted his skin open.

A Dom was right beside us flogging a sub on the Cross. He would look at me and I would smile before looking away. I wanted to play a cute, playful sub personality that enjoys teasing. I wanted to make him want me even more. I wanted to make sure he was hungry for me, but knew he couldn't have me. But, to be honest I rarely gave him attention and that was driving him nuts. He wasn't 100% into his scene and that made me not into it. I watched two chicks get harnessed for suspension. The spanking bench was totally hot. There was a couple into light spanking on a few things. The owner played with one of his girls by teasing her clit the whole time on a medical table, at times lightly choking, sometimes a light kiss...mainly building the tension. There was a flat surface much like a bed suspended from the ceiling and I wanted on that so bad! My mind was going wild with all the things someone could do to me on that surface. A couple occupied it almost the entire time we were there and my husband wasn't going to do anything. One guy kept getting right in front of me where ever I moved and grabbing hooks and handles on the ceiling. He pulled himself completely up. There was something that looked like a huge black spider web and my playful side wanted to explore... Truth... there were two swings - like playground swings, not sex swings - and watching a man swing a woman made me dripping fucking wet. The owner had a girl in one and he was in a position at her side like men use to propose to a woman. He was totally looking up at her with such adoration and playfulness, but there was such a tension and seriousness. The other was a Dom swinging a lady. There was nothing special about his actions. It was the same motion you would use to push anyone on a playground. I literally could have watched him swing her for hours. HOURS. We have to go back to the park - if for nothing other than you to swing me. The simple swing, simple action, care, playful, tension, the role definition... OMG I never knew such opposites could be found in a swing. I couldn't take my eyes off it. Even this early in the morning with very little sleep, I'm soaking wet just thinking about having you swing me.

My husband is trying to be supportive and not just bolt. I'm totally into it and he couldn't be more opposite. He thought the girl from the couple we met was decent so he wants to go back there. I want to go back if I get the sexy chill guy only and I won't, so I couldn't care less. My main excitement for play exists in the facility I'm currently in. I'm sorry my dear, sweet husband. There are other, better women he will want to fuck in the future. But, there isn't a place like this anywhere near where we live. I see he's anxious and I feel for him. I know that if you aren't into this, it can even be repulsive if it's too strong. Everyone's different and it's not his thing. That's fine. Since I decided I'd never lie to you, it was nice to have him there. It filled a soft Domme fantasy of mine to make him sit and watch things he can't handle without making an awful face, or saying "OMG", "there's no way", "seriously? People like that", "that had to hurt" etc. When I saw one hint of any of those it just took a look and he stopped flat. Some things I explained, some things I didn't. But, it also showed me a divide. I was bored at the first place - and even would have been after the sexy chill guy if I had gotten to him instead of being blocked by the pushy man - but a hint of "the other" and I light up like a kid at Christmas. I actually ran in the first place to get my husband so he could come watch with me because I was so excited. I enjoy playing most of the time, but I crave this. So, I left there biting the inside of my cheek to keep the tears pooling up and running down my cheeks. Clear as day... It's not a want. It's not an everyday thing. But, I actually NEED this. We were leaving to go back to the first place. It's give and take, respectful of both of our wants, but I wanted nothing more than to stay right there until the place shut down.

We walk back through the door at the first place. There are some decent single men, but I'm trolling for the one I want so I can see if he's still there. My husband has texted and the original couple has left, so I'm sure this guy has too. The pool tables are full of black men, so I pull my man into the couple room. I start kissing him and he likes to watch people. I wasn't having that. After watching what I did at the other place I just had to leave... nah. He's going to fuck me. I make him lie down and give him a great bj - tease him and ask if he's going to face fuck me. That's his favorite and I love pleasing. I tell him to lick me and it's really good. I still have my dress on zipped low and my tall boots. I order him to get up; I suck him a little more then tell him to strip and fuck me hard from behind - my favorite. He does as he's told and he's hitting it just right. I try my best to be as quiet as possible. I can't help but moan loud when he really gets into it. Next thing I know there's a hand inside my bra. I look over and there's a girl about my age maybe a couple of years younger attached to the hand grabbing my boob. I can't think too much because he's doing such a good job. I'm ready to cum, but I prolong it to see what she will do. She slides over and starts sucking my boob. I grab hers, pinch the nipple and we kiss for a while - she's good. She puts her head under me to get to my boobs, I finger her, her man is playing with my boobs and my man is fucking me. Mmmm fuck yeah! I'll take that. I didn't really look up much because I'm a focused person. Focus on the person or couple of people I want. Focus on who's playing with me at the time, hitting it hardest, or that I have the best connection with. She sits up and we never really stop kissing. Any chance we have to kiss, we take it. I ran my nails on her back and my man thrust in me hard. While I was reaching down for the base we were on top of, I touched the man's leg instead. Ok…no big deal. Well…it actually was. I knew I was at the edge of his leg and my hand had touched his cock, so my brain was focused there automatically. I was immediately calculating length and thickness. I picked my hand up to move it to the base. He grabbed it and put it on his cock. I'm kissing her, my man's watching all of this, and my hand is full of a thick, long (and after a few strokes I mentally note) curved cock. Mmmm… We scoot over for them to come in. It's then that I even look at the man. The chick was okay. She was blonde, good at everything so far, but not really my type. Then, I figured out why my man was hitting it so hard… I glanced up through heavy sexy lashes and saw a hot black man with sexy thick lips just like my baby. Daddy, you have the most amazing lips. I absolutely love kissing you until I can't breathe! I saw those lips and you registered in my head before the fact that he was black. I hesitated for a second, then long story short; we end up trading pretty quickly. I knew kissing him would be fun. I love it. There's nothing like kissing you and he should be a good fill in. With my eyes closed, it was easily you mmmm. He pulled my hair back, kissed my neck and bit at it. Yep, getting better. I push back on him and start sucking him within minutes. It only takes a second before he's rock hard and does a great job talking dirty :) I back off because I know he's close. I go full force the next time, fingers tight around the base, hand cupping and playing with his balls (HUGE) and my mouth bobbing before the twist everyone likes. I actually feel his cum racing up his shaft and immediately pull off. He throws his head back - tension was fucking high for him. I did that one more time. I swallowed that wide cock down my throat and he seems impressed. Just because I look like a prissy bitch doesn't mean I can't fuck if I'm in the mood to give it to you completely. When I come up, he reaches for a condom. We kiss and I know he wants me on my back - um…. no. I press my cheek into him and say, "Do you think you can fuck me hard from behind? I want to feel that hit me." He's happy to oblige. I go up on all fours and I know my man is LOVING the show because he's hard enough to be in the other chick right after he's fucked and cum inside me. No bj except mine could do that and he even said it was because I went after that black guy! Mmmm hehe. He's going in easy and I want it hard. I arch my back for him and he takes my hair easy, meticulously getting every hair then pulls it. Hell yeah. I push my ass up higher so he can go deeper and he pushes me forward to kiss his woman. I play with her boobs while kissing her with both men fucking us. I bet that would have been a good pic! He makes me cum a few times then puts me on my back. He pushes all his muscle into me and I love that pressure, always have. His arm goes under my neck and then the other. He kisses me and fucks me like that for a while. I can tell he wants to cum. He is into it, his muscles tighten and he slows to stop it. We go through that a few times and it's fun. He puts me on my side and it doesn't do anything. We kiss alot, he's back on top of me and then he pulls out. I know he wants me to suck it but I'm not into that. We go our separate ways…we go play pool again. No one worth playing with left, just one old dude that was a maybe. After playing pool, we came back here and fucked again while discussing the big, thick curved black man that had just fucked his wife. :)

CHAPTER 14

My Daddy Dom and I message almost every day throughout the entire day. We discuss work, area events, ways to improve everything under the sun, politics, sexy scenes we would like to play out, fantasies, daydreams, hot pictures we would like to take of each other, his past, how he grew up, how I grew up, triggers for us, what makes us tick, what's important to us and what we want. If there's something we can discuss, we've covered it. This man literally knows me inside and out. He doesn't judge me. He knows every want and every desire that runs through my kinky mind. The best part is that he's willing to try them.

It was about a year after I first met this man, when I asked him to send me an email of a fantasy he has. He asked for a little guidance on what I'm looking for in regard to a topic. I told him to send me a detailed fantasy you have. If you could have any fantasy in the world right now, which one would you pick? I was surprised when I opened my email and found the email below. That opened the door to us discussing other men. It's such a turning point. I'd also like to think he realized I was his even then!

I would love to teach you how to have the most intense orgasm of your life. I love to show you pleasures of the flesh you never knew existed. I am looking for a lady that wants to try new things and can relax and allow me to explore her body, bringing her to orgasm after orgasm. It would turn me on for you to moan and say, "Oh my god I did not know my body could do that". Below is a fantasy of mine that I would like to share with you: I am sitting in the lobby of a hotel; I get a text that says room 69. I go up to the room and find the door slightly open. When I enter I hear the shower running. I get undressed and go into the bathroom and pull back the shower curtain. I see you there totally naked; this is the first time we actually have met. I climb into the hot shower and French kiss you for a long time. You feel my cock getting hard. I then fuck your brains out in the shower but just before I explode I stop. I then pick you up and carry you to the bed where I find an assortment of toys, clamps rope etc. You spend the next few hours having one orgasm after another. After I have played with you, I then start to slowly fuck you. You reach up and squeeze my nipples;

I start to fuck you harder and faster. Finally I slam my cock in hard, keep it in deep, reach down and as I French kiss you, you feel my cock pumping cum deep inside you. Once done with the kiss we lay there exhausted.

Later, I take your hand and we move off the bed so that I can tie you up in a chair with your legs apart. I then put on you a blind fold and headphones. You can't see or hear anything. After about five minutes, you feel someone playing with your nipples and pussy. Then you feel a cock enter your pussy. Slowly then faster and harder your fucked, you cum. Then he pulls out. Then, you feel a different much larger cock slide into your pussy. You are fucked hard and fast and cum again. Then, that cock leaves and you're sitting there catching your breath. Then a third cock fucks your brains out, then a fourth and fifth. Your pussy is throbbing, sore and you're totally exhausted. After a few minutes I take off your blind fold and untie you. Nobody else is around. The only thing you see is a glass with many loads of cum. I hand the glass to you and ask you to either pour it all over your breasts and play with the cum or drink it all. You think about it and then.... After a while, we go down to the hotel bar where I tell you the 5 guys who fucked your brains out are at the bar.

So my husband's family will be keeping the kids this weekend. I know I have to email before playing. I don't know if I'll play or not, but I can't take my phone into the facility in one of the biggest metropolitan cities within the Southeast. I'm in the panties my Dom likes with black lace trim. Boots. Red lingerie piece that sets my boobs up high and my nipple jewelry is red. May check out a dungeon here if the club isn't fun.

We walk in, find a place to put our stuff and check out the club. It looks nice and the people are very friendly. I end up playing with a few people before the night is over. My husband enjoys watching me. We go back to the room, fall asleep in each other's arms, and wake up to make love.

Good evening, Sir. I decided I wanted to do a party Saturday night. I wore my black Fredericks dress, black boots, no bra, and my hair straight. I have on lots of mascara, dark gray eye shadow, and pink shiny lip-gloss. I chatted with a lot of people - more social than I usually am. Danced with a few. Met one single that was cute online and he turned out to be even better in person. My husband and I played with a couple. I played with a hot guy I wanted to meet up with and he literally never left my side all night awww so cute. Soccer player. Educated. Good looking. Good at playing. He had never played in a party room before and well he did. One guy that's into BDSM stuff but a creeper to me came in early while I was giving him a bj and told him to take my dress off me. Long story short he was excited, views from all angles, moaned and said "and people ask why we throw these parties… This… This is why… Damn!" He throws one of the parties there. I'm glad he was enjoying the show along with everyone else watching! The dude I was fucking was good. He left blood spots on my nipples from sucking so hard. We kissed and touched even at the party just being there. Amazing kisser. Danced with a few guys. A black guy taught me a dance, which I completely sucked at. And Seth and I played with a couple - she had H's ;) I miss you baby…

I went home and worked through the week like normal. I've been teaching the kids things that they wouldn't be learning for a couple more years. I want them to stay advanced, intelligent and hungry for knowledge. We go through the same, every day schedule of work, school and family activities. We always try to do something fun with our children. We take them on trips to Disney, the beach, see sporting events, experience new cultures, and try to attend a variety of seasonal festivals and events. Our children stay in the nicest of hotels, eat at lavish restaurants and experience things most adults never have! We try to teach them right from wrong, the golden rule and how to make decisions.

Today is play day with Daddy! We were just going to play like we usually do. I didn't wear cute panties like he likes. Today, I was in a hurry and my husband picked out granny panties for me to wear. The rule is that my husband needs to be wearing panties each time I meet my Dom to play. Well, like I said, we were in a hurry today. He did not wear panties and I wasn't in the mood to push for it. I arrive at the motel and put my things down. Within minutes, my Dom is in the room. We're fooling around a little bit and he lifts my tight dress up over my hips. My boots look amazing on my legs. My dress hugs every curve on my body, accentuating every sexy inch of me! He sees my granny panties and I look away. I know he's pissed. He immediately asks if my husband is in panties today. I'm thinking through my options. My Daddy Dom is pissed. I don't want to make it worse, but I'll never lie to him either. I simply reply, "No. No, he is not." His next phrase was, "and you're not in sexy panties either, are you?" I don't even look at him. I start to explain that we were running late this morning and we didn't have time, but he stopped me mid-sentence. "That's not what I asked, now is it?" I replied that it wasn't. I could feel my excitement and a bit of fear building within me. I was about to be punished. I deserved punishment for disobeying. What would he select? I explained that I wanted granny panties today because they're comfortable and I'm bleeding. I only wore pads then, so I needed something a little bigger than a thong. He said that he understood that, however that's not what I'd been instructed to do. So, he tells me to get up on the bed on all fours. My pulse begins to race and I do as I'm told. He spanks me multiple times while making me count each impact with him. I do as I'm told. Then, he says "baby, I understand you're being considerate of me while you're bleeding. However, there are plenty of things we can do during this time of the month." Oh

God! What does THAT mean?! I started running possibilities through my head, but he quickly showed me exactly what he meant. He tells me to pick my head up. He puts a cold weather outdoor facemask over my head and then tells me "face down, ass up." He spanks me a couple more times, then walks away again. I hear him open the curtains. Oh no! There were a lot of people outside! My initial reaction is humiliation, but I quickly realize he must know no one is there or he wouldn't have done it. He has to be as discreet as I do, so he wouldn't get himself into trouble! I feel something cold on my ass. He asks me if I remember what I was told to wear. I respond. He says, "and did you?" My only response was, "no Sir. I did not." He asks if I remember what my husband is supposed to wear while we play. I say yes and explain the item to him. He says, "and did you make sure he wore that today?" I felt like I had truly disappointed him. "No Sir. I didn't. I'm very sorry." He says, "Yes, you are. But, you'll learn quickly that when I say something I mean it and that you shouldn't test your Master. Understand?" "Yes Sir" I reply. My face has been pressed down into the mattress. He takes the once cold object off my ass and I'm still trying to figure out what it is. I hear him growling the words at me, "Listen carefully. Don't move. Don't move an inch. I'm very disappointed in my sub today. I can't let you get by with such disrespect. I asked for something simple and you couldn't follow my orders. Now, you must be disciplined." While the word disciplined moves across his lips, I feel a rough, harsh tug at the top of my panties. I feel tugging and yanking. The next things I feel are my Dom's fists on my ass at the top of my panty line. He's grabbed them! I hear the rip and I know the object was a knife. He's literally cutting these off of me! I can't see anything, but it's clear as day. He's made his point. I'm to NEVER show up in granny panties again! Now, I'm humiliated. I'm bleeding without any sort of protection at all and he doesn't care. He says, "I don't want you in these ever again" and with that, I'm completely naked. He tells me to flip onto my back. He face fucks me a bit through the open mouth hole in the mask. I can't see anything, but having my vision taken away from me has heightened all of my other senses. I can smell his skin against mine, the smell of menstruation, hear the growl in his voice a little more intense, and feel the increased moisture between my thighs due to him making me so wet. Lying on my back, he shows me exactly what other things we can do during this time of the month. With no preparation at all, he spits on my pussy and ass then slowly starts to enter my ass. I had no idea we would be doing anal that day! I'm so tight and it takes a while to work me before he can get all the way in. But, today he's decided to go all in with the first stroke. He fucks my ass, fills it with cum and goes to shower. I couldn't believe what had just happened! How am I supposed to get out of this room without panties or a pad or anything? I grew more infuriated while he was in the shower. He said bye, kissed me and left. I just sat there, panicking, trying to figure out how I can get out. I remember I have a pair of panties and a pad in my SUV, so I clean up and quickly run out to get it. I return to the room, shower, dress and leave. I'm pissed by the time I get in the vehicle. How the fuck could he do that to me? Just leave me there with nothing to wear out? What an ass! I'm driving around trying to let myself calm down when he finally messages a couple hours after he left the room. I tell him I'm pissed and he says, "You knew the rules. You didn't follow them. Be pissed." Fuck you dude! We don't message for a day and a half. In hindsight, it's my fault. At the time, I definitely didn't see it that way. But, looking from the outside in, I was still very turned on by how dominant he had been with his sexy sub! He now has me wear tampons at his request every time I experience that time of the month. We even talked through what I should buy because I had no experience with them. But, my Daddy knew. He even helped his wife back in the day! It's so nice having someone that knows about everything as a Dom, sub and lover!

I always said I would never mix play with anyone from work. And it happened. Not once, not twice, not three times, but so far four times after swearing I won't do it. One wasn't necessarily my fault. He ended up at the swingers club I usually attend. We had both been drinking a lot and one thing led to another. When I woke up the next morning, my husband was replaying every illicit detail of my evening. Included in the recap was how this man fucked me. Oops. We had been friendly at work, but never crossed a professional line into flirting. That line is gone now.

Another was a sexy female that I just always had the feeling she plays. She never said it. I just get that feeling around others of my kind! She brought up playing one day and the conversation led to all sorts of juicy details being divulged. She had always fantasized about having sex with another woman, but didn't find one that was attractive she would want to fuck. As soon as she learned that I enjoy the lifestyle, she decided she wanted it to be me! Who am I to tell her no? We are the same level at work, so there shouldn't be any issues there. Her husband doesn't know she plays, let alone that she craved the touch of a woman. So, long story short, one day we both met up and she explored her wildest fantasy! She's a natural! We both had a great time!

My lover and I were set to meet one morning to play. We spent the two days before it planning what activities, outfits and implements we would need for the day. The scenes were fully discussed and we were both primed for our session. We were so excited sending filthy, dirty messages back and forth for days. Then, the evening before, she says she's not going in to work the next day. Wtf?! I swear she has radar! I think it's important for him to spend time with his family when he can, so it's fine. I'd be lying if I didn't admit my immediate reaction was a small trickle of tears down my cheek. I was irritated about it when I first woke up the next morning, but decided to have a positive perspective for the day. We chatted and he told me how disappointed he was. I explained that I needed to stay positive or I'd probably go off, so we changed the topic pretty quickly. I was sad. I wanted my Master. And, I know he needed me. Gah, it sucks!

While we are on the topic, nothing is perfect! We've had the battle over and over and over again about how we don't get to spend enough time together. It's happened so many times that I finally left him because I couldn't take feeling like I didn't matter anymore. While I see that it's the situation and not that he didn't care or want to see me or even try to see me, it was still too much to take! I asked him not to ever message me again and delete every photo he had of me. I was done! I cried nonstop for days. I would even sit at my desk at work and cry. My heart was broken and there was nothing that could fix it, not even time. After four or five days, he messages me. I was less than loving and polite. I had a fury burning in me. The next few days were rough, honest and therapeutic. There's nowhere else I can be than being his. I own this man. He owns me. My day starts with checking for messages from him and ends with falling asleep chatting with him. We agree to try to it again, but I know we're both being cautious.

A few days later we had a great opportunity arise. He said he could let me know by 7:00 that morning if he could play. It doesn't always work like that. I know if we can play at different times or a few days in advance. I typically leave before that, so I knew it may draw attention from those that watch our children if I drop them off late. My husband handled the situation and went in late that morning. Still nothing. I got dressed, climbed in my SUV and left my house. I didn't bring any sexy outfits or toys because I assumed he couldn't meet. He messages me when I get halfway between my house and the city we were going to meet in. He's available and I'm past ready to play with my Daddy! I had another play date scheduled for that morning with a successful attorney. I decide to cancel that with a quick message while I'm messaging my Daddy and a sexy well-built BBC. Such a fun morning's drive! I'm now heading to the typical hotel we use. He's on his way and I cannot wait to feel him on top of me. The weight of my Daddy covering every inch of me is pure bliss. In a matter of minutes I will be engulfed in Daddy kisses that will set my body on fire. I want him. I need him. I walk into the room and it is as cold as Antarctica. Who the hell stayed here in this cold room the day before? A penguin? I strip off my clothing down to just my bra, leave the door unlatched and go hibernate under the covers. I leave my bra on because it is a black lace sexy push up that makes my tits look amazing, and it keeps my pierced nipples warmer in this arctic room! He walks in. Puts his stuff down. He's in the black t - shirt and blue jeans I love to see him wear. There's just something about that combination! He walks around to the other side of the bed and leans over me to kiss me. Mmmmmm Daddy. Perfect, big, soft lips. A sexy goatee that's never coarse or prickly. Cheeks smooth as silk since he just shaved. I slip into a state of delight. It feels so normal yet so erotic and intriguing. My Master kisses me harder, deeper, exploring my mouth with his tongue. His entire body is over me and his face has mine pressed into the pillow. It's as if he could never get enough of kissing me no matter how hard or deep or breathtaking it is. I feel my slit moisten while we're lip locked. My back arches and I wrap my arms around his neck. My God! This man just walked in the door and I've completely been taken over by him. That day he teaches me the beautiful, painful joys of feeling a cane whack my ass. One swat registers the bliss and pure unadulterated pain. I'm a pain slut through and through. I enjoy it. I'm searching for that one thing, that one activity, which will break me. I feel the second strike of the cane and I feel myself jerk. I try to remain perfectly still, but I wasn't ready for that one. I start thinking about my Dom. How sexy he is. How much I love him. How I want to please him. How he's pushing me because it will turn him on to see my ass with cane stripes and because I've asked for this. He's really doing this for me. It takes such a strong man to hurt someone they've developed feelings for and I'm thankful he can provide what I need. I end up with somewhere around 15 stripes when I must have moved in an odd manner. He rubs my ass and says "babygirl, are you okay?" I say no and ask for just a minute. I've been in subspace. I ask for a minute to come back to reality. I feel tears slowly escaping the corners of my eyes. He comforts me and I cry for a moment, then when I've calmed I ask for a little more. He tells me I will get 6 more and I count with him. My Master kisses the broken skin on my ass and I am trying to suppress the tears. He crawls up beside me and cuddles me. Mmmm my Master. That afternoon it was more like making love than being ravaged. And after the caning I took, that felt perfect to me. With my breasts, ass and neck covered in hickies, love bites and cane marks I was on cloud nine.

That evening I was seductively undressing when I asked my husband to look at my ass. I had beautiful cane marks all over me that turned from a lustful, passionate red to a deep purple color within a day. Every time I turned over in bed that night or sat down too quickly at work, I would have a sharp, painful reminder of the carnal explorations of our last meeting. The open wounds were starting to heal a couple of days later. That was the same day we went to a very public pool. My entire family went with me. I have an amazing ass and I could feel people staring at it, and the bruises peaking out from the bottom of my swimsuit, the entire day. My mother saw the hickie on my neck because I wore my hair up in a sexy messy bun. I like to play with fire. I wanted someone to call me out on it and ask who gave it to me. My clit was throbbing with the excitement of someone coming up behind me and commenting on the hot bruises on the top of my tits. But no one did, because I live in the bible belt of the South. Some gave me the sexy glare like they knew exactly how I got them and that it wasn't from my husband. Then, their wives usually made them go to another area of the water park.

I am meeting my lover today and I'm in a very submissive mood! Today, I need my Dom! He knocks on the door to the hotel and locks my lips in a kiss before I can even shut the door. I say, "Hello Master" so that he knows I fully expect him to be Dominant with me during our play. He places his bag on the table and looks through the items in my bag. I'm excited and ready to submit to his every desire. To be honest, I know a lot happened that day. I can only remember one thing. He wanted me to suck him; and I love doing that! He orders me to move my head to the edge of the bed and let it hang off the side. In my mind, I was a little reluctant. He yanks me down the bed and now my shoulders are hanging off too. I am surprised by his actions and hope that he will be rough the entire time. My Master lowers his balls onto my face and tells me to lick them. I don't have much choice! I can either lick and hopefully breathe, or be completely smothered by them. I do as I'm told and I hear him begin to moan. I am so happy he's pleased! He places his cock on the tip of my lips and I know what he wants, but it's hard to such him when my head is so low. I work feverishly to make him hard. He's rock solid and ready. He pulls out and slaps me in the face with his dick. The next time, he plunges deep inside me while holding my head up. I think it's sweet until I realize he only did it so that he can roughly fuck my face. He's so rough I can barely breathe! He allows me a minute to breathe and gain composure while he calls me his good girl. Mmm… My head is swimming in pleasure. I lay back down and he enters my mouth again. With the same rough speed, he continues to use me as nothing more than a hole. He pushes all the way in and holds it there. Seriously?! I start to panic. Is he really going to choke me with it? I can't breathe! I try to pull my head down to get off him and breathe, but he doesn't allow it. I pull harder and the man decides to show me his dominance. He says, "babygirl, you're going to suck me and I'm going to stay deep in your throat until I decide I'm ready to let you breathe. Do you understand?" I nod and respond, "Yes Sir." He begins slowly, but I know it won't last long. When he's all the way in I swear I can't breathe. I begin panic again. I try to calm myself down and trust the man I handed over my body to long ago. I submit to him. He's my Dom. He's not going to let anything happen to me. Most importantly, I'm extremely wet! I want this! He must be counting or holding his breath that long too so that he knows how to time it just right. I can tell he's on a power high and I love it. The next few times, he stays in my throat longer blocking every chance of me getting a fraction of a second of air. I can always tap out if I need to or use a safeword when I can get air and speak, but that's not something I want. The last time, I slip into subspace. He's deep in my throat giving me every inch of him and he's placed the palms of his hands tightly on the outside of my throat. He's choking me from the inside and outside! He's controlling my air, whether I live or die, and definitely my orgasm. Maybe it's the lack of oxygen to my brain.

Maybe it's the pure bliss of being so turned on and pleasing him so much. Maybe it's the mix of it all. Whatever it is, I live in this beautiful, glorious state of subspace for a good 15 minutes. I have never experienced anything so amazing! We finish playing and he fucks me well like he always does. We both leave satisfied, but always wanting more of each other.

It's 5:30 a.m. and my eyes are barely starting to flitter open. Why did I stay up so late chatting? I make a mental note to get at least two decent nights of sleep a week. I know I want nothing more than to hide under the covers for the rest of the day, but I enjoy success too much. I wait until my husband turns off our snooze timer. It's so nice that he gets ready first. My loving husband wakes me up by saying, "Good morning beautiful" and gives me a quick kiss almost every morning. I'm so fortunate. We have the best marriage, wonderful children, and a perfect life. I reach for my phone while he's turning on the water for his shower so that I can check the time. I see a message from my lover waiting for me on my screen. My heart skips a beat! Now I'm awake! He's better than a massive shot of caffeine. My normal habit every morning is to push the button on my very popular brand of smartphone to see if I have a message from my Dom. Before I fully realize where I am, what my name is, or what day it is, I check my phone. I see a message I missed from our conversation last night. I must have fallen asleep around 1:30 a.m. I feel a huge smile spread across my face as I begin to remember the conversation full of the kinky things we were chatting about. Now that I'm awake the important tasks of the day are starting to mix in with the sexy thoughts. GAH! I guess that means it's time to get up. I walk to the shower, kiss my husband in our master bathroom, and then he swats my ass as I walk by him. While in the shower, I plan my workday. I'm ready to take on the world and climb the ladder of success. I'm a young driven professional. I know it won't be easy to climb the ladder in my corporate world, but I'm willing to work hard to show I'm capable. I massage my hands across the back of my neck to work out the lack of sleep. I wash across my pierced nipples and a tingle of excitement runs straight to my clit. Forget work! I want to stay home and fuck all day. I'd love to have him kissing all over me within a few hours. But I can't, not today. I have big meetings today and then my children have soccer practice. We have a beautiful home with the wonderful morals of the southern Bible belt with families that are professional, successful, and very well respected. Everyone knows us, even if we don't know him or her. That makes it very difficult to enjoy my carnal desires that are only fulfilled by being a swinger and having my love of BDSM explored and pushing every limit possible. Now I realize I'm feverishly massaging my clit in the shower. I'm already slippery from the one message from him I read this morning. My little daydream has taken me to another level and I'm about to cum. I lean against the cold tile and let the hot water run across my body as the orgasm runs through me. Mmmm…it's going to be a great day!

CHAPTER 15

I'm dedicated to my work. I'm very type A. I'm dominant, sexy, intelligent and sweet - a lethal combination. I may be working on a project at work for a couple of hours and then my mind wanders. What's he doing? Wonder what color panties he would have picked to wear today? Would he have been the Dom today if we were playing? Would I be caned?

I wake up early. My husband has to nearly threaten me to get me out of bed. I'm tired from being up late chatting with my lover. I know I have a jam-packed morning at work that I can't skip out on, so I slowly make my way to the shower. Halfway through the shower, I'm awake. "I get to play with him today!!!" That phrase has my pulse racing and now I'm excited to get the day started. The faster I get through my tasks at work, the faster I can get to him. We get the kids ready and drive to work together. I drop him off at his company and head on to mine. I'm practically giddy! I stop at a drive-thru to grab a light breakfast and drink before getting to work. Phone call after phone call, I'm running behind on the schedule I had planned out for the morning in my head on the drive to work. He and I message some and I am so turned on that it's literally everything I can do to not just walk out the door. I finish just before lunchtime and run down the stairs to my vehicle. I jump inside and speed to the low-grade motel. Never in my wildest dreams did I ever imagine I'd ever step foot inside one of these establishments. For those wondering what a successful professional thought of the business, the staff at the one I use is always friendly, efficient and the rooms are always cleaner than I expect! I message him to let him know where I am and the room number. I ask him to stop and get a drink for me as I plan to skip lunch. There's no telling what crazy stuff I may end up doing so an empty stomach sounds like a better idea than any gagging or vomiting. I turn the water on for a quick rinse in the shower and my phone lights up with the message "do you think the girl working the drive-thru knows I'm wearing pink lace panties?" I giggle and reply, "no I doubt she does, but you can unzip a little or pull them up over the top of your jeans and show her if you'd like." I know he won't do it, but I would do something like that. I'm drying off and have one leg in the sexy new stockings I just purchased when he knocks on the door. I make him wait while I get the other one on, my ultra high leopard print stripper heels he bought me and a simple black silk robe. I look sexy and he'll definitely be excited when he sees me. I know it's uncomfortable for him to wait outside the door. Someone may recognize him and then this could all be over, but I make him wait like a good boy.

When I open the door, the rush of passion runs through me. I've known this man for four years and I get that same feeling every single time I see him. He puts his stuff down and wraps himself around me, enveloping me in a deep kiss. "Right here" I think to myself "right here feels perfect!" He's much taller than I am, but I'm closer in these heels. He almost knocks me off balance, so I order him to strip completely naked. We kiss again. There's no space between us, no second taken for breathing. It's that all encompassing, lose yourself in the moment type of kissing most people only see in the movies. If I don't stop this, I'll never play and just kiss all day. I tell him to come to the bed with me, but first show me what he's brought. All his toys are now laid out in front of me; he's brought rum for the first time, beer for him, various sodas that may be used to fuck my pussy and a funnel. I'm very careful to be responsible and never do anything unless I trust someone. I've never had a drink with him. Ever. He's heard about how I am, but never experienced it. I lay my filters to the side and all inhibitions are gone. I am completely the woman I'm meant to be. Doing what I feel and saying what I want to say, I lay all apprehensions down and fully experience things without worrying about my the status that comes along with my last name, what image I have to portray or who I need to please.

I throw back a few shots of the rum he brought. I haven't had this particular kind of rum. I drank so many shots of liquor that I lost count. The room wouldn't stop spinning! I planted my pussy on his face and told him the only way I'd get off of him so he could breathe was if he tapped out. Mmmm it was such a powerful position to be in that day. He licked my pussy and ass while he tongue fucked both. He ate me out so well. Even though I was tipsy, I was completely focused on making Samson serve me. I opened my thighs up away from his ears and raised my cunt off his mouth while I stroked his cock slowly. It drove him crazy. I explained that he would be struggling for air. And that the next time he attempted to tap out, it wouldn't work. If he ever wanted to breathe, he needed to bite me to break through to his Domme. I didn't think there was any way for his cock to get any harder, but it grew longer and thicker. Facesitting was apparently high on his list of turn ons. I knew how much he wanted my mouth on his cock. I knew how aroused he already was. So, I'd lean forward while I smothered him with my thick thighs and juicy cunt. I teased the hell out of him and denied him the opportunity to cum. Mmmm the filthy, nasty, erotic things I said to him. I was talking shit to him and he loved it. He was hard as a rock! I rode his cock hard. I wanted it! It was hot as fuck! He had the opportunity to fuck my pussy the way I like it. This man has one position no other man has mastered yet and I loved feeling him in me. He hit my g spot perfectly! After a few minutes of that I decided my sub needed to see his Domme in all her glory. I walk over to the toys I laid out when I arrived and put on my strapon harness. I knew it turned him on to see me prepare to fuck his ass. I lay on the bed beside him and he sat up. I threw my foot on the back of his neck and slammed his face into the bed. I said, "What the fuck do you think you're doing? I don't remember telling you to get up!" I had his neck pinned under my foot. It was intoxicating to see him in that position under me! Next, I showed him his options of various sizes and colors of dildo that would fuck his ass □ . I went to the front of the bed and knelt down in front of him. I asked him if he liked the huge 13" black option that is as thick as a man's arm or if he wants something a little smaller. He lifted his head off the mattress and opened his mouth for the 13" to be inserted. Holy fuck!!! I didn't know anyone could fit that in his or her mouth! I was speechless! He's my submissive. He wanted cock in his ass. My pussy was dripping wet while I watched him suck on an enormous BBC! I pulled it out of his big sexy lips and asked if he wanted the 9" or the 7" attachment. He said, "maybe the 7" first and then try the 9" attachment." I said, "hmm okay." I felt so powerful with a cock attached to me. I loved watching him suck my cock. Pushing his head down on it was exciting, but when I would hold his head down until he would gag almost made me cum! I grabbed the lube and spread it across his manpussy. I wanted him on his back so he saw my face while I fucked his hole. I started playing with the 9" at his opening. I knew it was entirely too large for him. But, I had to do it. Up until this point, I hadn't ever completely let go and been Domme, but today was the day he got the woman of his dreams! I got half of the 9" in him before it was too much. I was proud of him, so I switched to the 7" cock. It slid right in him. I think he wanted it and I had purposely started with the larger size so the smaller one would feel amazing inside him. I jacked his dick a few times, and then ordered him to get up. When I stand, I almost fall in my heels. I'm drunk. I'm a FemDom. And, I own him. Literally. I told him to open his legs wide and bend over the bed. Hehehe he was such a sissy slut. He loves having his ass fucked by his Domme. He loves being owned, submissive, challenged, pushed, and MINE! I fuck his ass that day and feel the full weight of my role. I smile such a mischievously evil grin when I realize I am finally, fully his Dominatrix. I push in him and tell him not to fucking move. I pour myself another shot of rum with one hand, which I end up sloshing everywhere. I make a mess and I don't fucking care. His ass feels amazing and so do I. His hole opens up wide for me. I pull my dick out to see how he's stretching for me. Mmmm…that is hot. I hit it harder, deeper, faster and I sipped on my shot. I wish I had that on video because I knew it had to be the hottest thing I've ever done. I was dripping wet down my strapon, down my thighs, and dying to have his cock in me. But, it wasn't time yet. I ordered him to stroke his little clit. I wanted it hard so he could fuck me and please me. I tapped his balls a few times just to watch him jump. CBT is so hot! I swear it felt like I was being rammed every time I hit my cock into his manpussy. I totally got off on it and I knew everyone in the building heard me cum when I was finally done fucking his ass. I pulled it off and told him to fuck me. My Daddy Dom has never disappointed me, even when he was in his submissive subspace. He went straight to the position only he can fuck me in and I came harrrrrd on his cock! Over the next thirty minutes or so, he put me in a few different positions until he grunted and erupted within my pussy. I loved feeling him unload his seed deep in me! That day was the first time in over four years that I've called him by his submissive given name. He earned it. We both earned our titles that day.

We cuddled for a while and then he went to shower. Our room reeked of sex and I was past tipsy. Our toys were thrown all around the room and I didn't see how there was any possible way I could drive. At least I was being responsible! I sent my husband a text while my lover was in the shower. I told him to meet me at the motel room because I knew driving was a bad idea. My sexy lover comes out, gets his stuff packed up, kisses me a couple of times and leaves. My husband came out 10 minutes later, loving the sight of me laid out all across the mattress. I giggled because I knew he enjoys fucking me most fun I'm fun and carefree. So, my husband took round two that day. After a hot, hard romp, he packed my things up while I stumbled to the counter. I had never been this drunk before during a play session. My lover brought out an extreme side to me that I became addicted to. We made it down the steps and I giggled the whole way to the vehicle. At least I made it in! That night we went to soccer practice for one of our children. He took a fold out chair and placed it in the grass so I had somewhere to sit and watch. I was still buzzed and I knew I was rocking a mom of the year title. I pulled off an efficient day of work, rough kinky play, and now soccer with my family at a church. Jesus, I hope I don't go to hell. But, I am super woman. I can do it all. And, I just proved that. The best part was, no one had any idea. They thought I was the sweetest person they had ever met!

CHAPTER 16

Sometimes I wonder if this is an addiction. I honestly love having sex and could do it all day every day! I never get tired of it; unless the person I'm having sex with is boring! Instead of calling it an addiction, I call it my favorite hobby. Some people golf, some people shop, and some people play the tables at a casino. I, however, pick sex each and every time I have someone that meets my standards to fuck over any other hobby. Keep in mind; this is when I have free time away from my little ones. Nothing takes time away from my family. I think you could accurately say it's an obsession. It also feeds into my competitive side. I want to be the best! I'm sure someone is better at every sex act than I am, but I haven't run into her yet. Don't think I'm a jealous bitch! If there is someone better, I'm just going to have her teach me her tricks!

Morning Daddy~

I've been added to a group chat. Drama abounds which is typical in a group chat, so I left. I was added to another group chat and I chatted with a couple of men. One told me he has access to boardrooms at a very upscale hotel in our area. I immediately knew which one he was talking about because it is beautiful! I love playing in the rooms there. I've never had an opportunity to play in a meeting room or on a boardroom table. He posted a picture in the group message and I started flirting. In all the parties I've been to and websites I've been on, I haven't seen this man. I had no idea how old he was, what he looked like, what turned him on or anything else. We discussed when we both might be able to play and I was free right then. It was late in the evening, but we had a sitter. It was the perfect time to take advantage of a quick, sexy, anonymous fuck. For the last 5 or 6 months I had been a good girl. I had played with my Dom and my husband, but that was about it. I hadn't had much free time and I'd focused much more on family life. I'd been very driven at work, which is very rewarding, but my slutty side had been buried for too long!

I messaged this guy back and told him he needed condoms to play with me. He responded that he didn't have any. I messaged my lover Samson. I began to report what I was wearing down to every sexy tiny little detail. I told him where I would be as required each time I play. I like to think he's protective of his babygirl and that he gets turned on knowing what I look like when I walk in to meet some random stranger that is about to fuck me hard. I stopped at a nearby gas station and purchased condoms quickly, then went over to the swanky hotel. He told me which entrance to use and I found a quiet place to wait. I checked that there were no security cameras anywhere. We looked at the boardroom in the picture, but the cleaning crew was working on it. We entered into another large, beautiful, theater style seating conference space. While I thought it was nice, it was not a boardroom table. He said, "There's one more we can get into without anyone seeing us. It has a nice leather couch and a small table." I was all about that. I followed in behind him. We kept the lights off and I turned the flashlight feature of my phone on so we could see. The last thing I wanted was for someone to see a light on in a space that should be empty. I always think 15 steps ahead. I put my necklace and phone on the table, and then started kissing him. Mmmm it was such a pleasant surprise, he could actually kiss. The half circle leather couch looked so supple. I couldn't wait to have my body stretched out across it. I started unbuckling his belt. I asked him what rules his rules are and he said no marks. Obviously this man was a married man. He didn't want marks because he didn't want to get caught by his wife when he returned home to his wife. This man looked a decade younger than his actual age, tall and attractive. I dropped to my knees to suck him. He seemed to enjoy my lips around his cock. He pulled me off so that he didn't finish in my mouth. He kissed me and played with my breasts, easy at first then hard as if he was kneading them. He said, "Why don't you take that off so I can see that pussy." I stripped immediately. My pants and panties went flying across the room and I sat down on the luxurious couch. He pushed my thighs apart and flicked the tip of my clit with his tongue. In seconds his entire face was in my pussy eating me out. When he started sucking on my clit, I purred and opened my legs into a wide high V over my head. He started fingering me and I pushed his hand away. That didn't stop him at all. He pushed his face and fingers back in me and I came quickly. My slit was so slippery and I wanted him inside me. He suggested we 69, so he laid flat on his back on the floor. I didn't hesitate! I crawled a sexy, slow, seductive crawl over to him and threw one thigh over his face. I positioned my pussy over his lips and slowly lowered myself onto them. I could tell he loved how sweet I tasted. It was like he couldn't get enough. I began sucking his cock, but I was distracted by how well he was licking me. I said, "you like a little face sitting, huh?"He was moaning mmmmhmmm against my pussy lips. I sat up off his face and said what was that in a playful tone. He said, "Yes, mmmm I do!" So I quickly sat down flat on his face and he was sucking harder. Deeper.

After a few minutes of that, I was ready to be fucked. I said, "I want your cock in me. Does doggy work for you? I like to be hit deep from behind." Would any man with a sexy woman sitting on his face have said no to that? He agreed that position would be good, so I bent over the back of the leather couch, spread my legs into a sexy V, and pushed my ass up as high as it would go in the air. I let him thrust for a while before I started pushing my hungry little cunt back into him. His two-way radio went off and I stopped. I didn't want someone to walk in on us, so I made sure he didn't have to go and then started talking dirty with him. He pushed on my lower back with one hand and grabbed my ponytail with the other. He pulled my hair so tight and he had my back arching just like he said he likes. He told me how much he loved my pussy and how lucky my husband was to have such a sexy wife. I giggled and said thank you. I asked if he wanted to spank me. He replied that he definitely wanted to, but with people in the next room and in the hallway he said it might be too loud. This stranger commented on my sexy ass and how he never actually expected to get a chance to fuck me. With that, I pushed back faster onto his cock. I wanted to milk cum out of his cock and listen to his manly growls as he unloaded in me. I came hard on him and a few minutes later he finished, too. We both got dressed and kissed again before we left the conference room. I reminded him that he needed to clean his face before he goes home because him entire face tasted like my pussy. Mmmm fuck.

I walk back out to the SUV. My husband is waiting on me. We drive about three minutes down the road. I've been telling him about my fun little romp. He says you need more don't' you. Why yes, I do actually. He says, "We could just pull over right here and fuck on the side of the interstate." I say ok and he says, "yeah right, you wouldn't do that." I said, "Try me. Your slutty wife needs cock. Let's fuck." So he finds an overpass and pulls under it. I explain he needs to watch for policemen and all the kind caring type of people in the South that usually stop to help when there are people with car issues. He tells me to get over there and suck his cock. I do and he's telling me how naughty I am and spanking my ass. There are cars flying by us. He gets out with cars flying by him. He opens my door and tells me to pull my pants down and bend across the passenger seat. That's when he realizes I'm not wearing any panties now. He slides in and starts with a smooth slow rhythm. Large trucks and small sports cars zoom past us. His balls are hitting my clit with each thrust and I love how that feels. My husband's cock is 2 full inches shorter than the one that just fucked me, but it's the perfect length, thickness and curve to satisfy me every time. I start screaming after a few thrusts. I can tell he loves this. He grabs my hips hard and picks up the pace. His dirty fucking slut of a wife just got used and he wouldn't have it any other way. I can hear how loud I am and I don't care. I cum hard on him and then he uses me to jack his dick off inside my hot, filthy slutty cunt. He fills me full of his sticky load and I'm not riding home with a cunt full of cum. What a fucking night this was! I need this more often. My inner whore is wide-awake now.

My Dom is very excited! Samson messages me asking questions about every little detail. I message him everything I just told my husband. He's proud of his babygirl for going out and having a little fun, especially while her hubby waits in the vehicle for her. A few days later we were able to clear literally just a few minutes in our schedule to see each other. As we were in wide, open public view, we couldn't do much of anything. The risk is very high since he does not have permission from his wife to even message other women, let alone meet or fuck. I've sent him sexy pics of my pretty bright pink lace panties all morning. I knew that would make him run his hands between my thighs and I was right! He's standing at my window while I'm in the SUV. He runs his hands between my thighs and starts caressing the top of the lace. It's everything I can do not to pull this man through my window, kidnap him and go play forever on some remote island. I can't do much without being seen, so I reach up and run my thumb across his bottom lip. My God those lips! I run my hand down his arm and we're chatting. A little playful small talk really so it will be easier to cover if someone we know walks up quickly. I want to kiss him. I'm laser focused on getting those lips on mine, but I know there is a strong possibility of people watching. He asks what I'm thinking and I tell him I want to kiss you. He agrees and I say "but you're not going to let me are you?" with a pouty expression across my face. There's a huge risk to it, but playing with fire seems to be a specialty of mine. He says the same thing I was thinking by saying, "I know me too. It will have to be quick." Mmmmmmm those lips… I could kiss them all day and feel like he just started kissing me and that I could kiss him forever without stopping all at the same time. My pulse quickened before I pulled up to met him. But after that kiss, I knew my pulse had to be skyrocketing. I had on a sophisticated dress that hugs my boobs, ass and is professional. However, I hiked it up pretty high on my thigh. I wanted to tease him. It's obviously working. He grabs the inside of my thighs and I have body butter on them. My legs are smooth and silky. He squeezes my entire thigh hard, leaving it aching hours later. He pinches the inside of my thigh. Why didn't I just make him get in the SUV? He told me later that night that he was really excited to see me that day. He also asked if I thought he wouldn't notice how I'd pulled my dress up high to show more leg. Hehe I didn't know if he would or not, but I know what my Daddy, lover, and sub enjoys.

We've discussed the daydream of running away together. While we're both highly intelligent rational people that understand what we'd be risking, that doesn't mean we can't enjoy the daydream. We love our spouses and our children very much. But, this obviously isn't just a one-time fling. Would things be different if our children weren't all under the age of 10? Maybe. Or, maybe it would be exactly the same as it is now! Whatever it is, his typically phrase "always" applies here. This man has changed me forever. In today's daydream we are at a nude beach. We go play around in the water and enjoy feeling our bodies soak in the hot summer sun while we're laying on the white sand. It couldn't be more perfect. When we're too hot, we go run down to the water again. He's chasing after me and catches me a few steps into the refreshing cool temperatures wrapping around us. After a quick kiss, I see him look to the side and I follow his glance. There's a sexy, tan, built, 20 something guy staring at us. My lover turns his attention back to me. Kissing my neck. Smacking my ass. Biting my neck. That's when I knew he's putting on a show to tease this potential playmate. And, it works. Within minutes, the guy has slowly made his way over to us and begins to introduce himself. We're all laughing and enjoying each other's company. Then, I watch them both lower their bodies into the water so that only their heads are visible. I feel a hand slip between my thighs toward my slit and instantly stop. I shoot mine a stare and he's got such a sexy look in his eye. It clicks for me. These two have already agreed through some non-verbal communication that our new friend has been given the green light. While my mind is processing all of this, his fingers dance along the curve of my ass. We move apart and act like we're just having fun enjoying a beach day. But we can all only stay apart a few moments. They both take turns fingering me. I stroke both of their massive cocks. I'm slippery even though I'm in water. My lover can see the need in my eyes. He tells the bartender that he needs to see how amazing I feel on his cock. I'm not sure he finished the sentence before I felt him push in me. I had to wrap my legs around him to keep from falling under the water. So for the next 30 minutes, those sitting on the beach near us watch as my two incredibly hot, tall, tan studs use every hole and leave cum dripping out of me. It's running down my thighs on my walk to our spot in the sand. We enjoy the rest of the afternoon with my legs spread wide for everyone to see the cream oozing out.

After we arrive back to our room, we shower and get ready for a night out. Typically we would go to a restaurant with an amazing sunset view and have quite a few drinks to get the night going. We walk over to a local nightclub and he has me bend over to pick up the keys he purposely dropped. My lover is one of a kind. He has me dressed in a very low cut, short dress with nothing underneath. He wants to show me off. He wants everyone to see how lucky he is, what an amazing woman he owns in BDSM and he definitely wants them to want her every time they look at her. He has his hand on my hip and steals a passionate kiss. I can feel a few eyes staring at us, which only triggers my exhibitionist side. He runs his hand up my thigh exposing part of my ass so that everyone will know there's nothing under the dress. We end up chatting with an attractive couple and he invites them back to our room. For the rest of the evening, we explore every position and possible hedonistic combination. I'm tired, worn out, sore and extremely satisfied. They leave. We fall asleep covered in the sweat, cum, piss and yes even a tear or two that was shed during our escapade.

Our other daydreams vary. They've been trips to swingers clubs and dungeons along with every sexy detail of what we would like to do while we're there. Some clubs and dungeons I've been too, he has not. I have the opportunity to throw in real life experiences of these locations to turn him on even more. Other times, we are cuddled together on the couch. Just cuddling together on a couch while watching TV. I always thought that sounded so boring. I was the type that never wanted to cuddle and if someone wanted that, I wouldn't play with that person. Now, I want cuddling with him. I asked if it was crazy and he always says something along the lines of "no babygirl, that's just part of it in this. It's not the same as everything else." Or, he'll say, "No it's not crazy. I'd like doing that too." We've discussed him moving in with my husband and I. We've discussed him having his own place and not being married to her. How I'd come over a few nights a week and stay with him. That's the best compromise I could get from my husband and I know he would need time with his child too, so it would work well. But it's all just a fantasy, right? Sometimes the daydream is that he is crawling through dirt, mud, leaves, twigs and ends up filthy. I have a collar around his neck showing my ownership. I tie him to a tree. He's wearing a stainless steel cage, which gets very warm in the sunlight. I've written all sorts of degrading things across his chest. Spit in his face. Kissed him so hard that he's poking me with that cage. Straining for release that he will never find while he's wearing it. I make him greet anyone that comes down the waterway in a boat, purposely humiliating him. Mmmm…he is such a good boi. He's a gentleman and core values must always stay intact while doing a scene, so it's only proper that he greet them. After all, this is the South. We have manners! Well, who said that this one would stay a daydream?

CHAPTER 17

Today's daydream was a trip. Somehow we would find time, he would be able to have a cover story for his wife and I would have my husband at home watching our children. It never matters where we would go in the fantasy because we always get super turned on by the end. I think I ended up flashing people in a grocery store, driving down the interstate and at dinner by the time he was done. I've actually done some of those in real life, but I'm not saying which ones! As far as the trip, will this ever happen? Probably not. I've tried to go with him on two rare work trips he had without her and his agenda was so jam packed with work that I wouldn't have been able to see him anyway. It's a goal of mine. I want it. Overnight. Somewhere we won't get caught. Able to breathe a little and see how much fun we could have turning some of the daydreams into reality.

While I'm chatting with him about this amazing trip that has my pussy dripping from the thought of us bringing back a sexy BBC or a chick to devour for the rest of the evening, I'm texting my husband. I tell him how wonderful he will do at work today in the very important meetings he has scheduled. I tell him how proud I am of him and how hard he's worked lately. I also work on my department's budget at work with multiple interruptions from an employee that cannot figure out how to correct an issue that needs to be resolved immediately. Can I multi-task? Damn straight. I work very hard to keep up the appearance that I'm a sophisticated businesswoman, loving wife and mother and active member of multiple communities. No one has any idea of the things you're reading. You may be reading this and pass by me in a hallway or sit in the same meetings with me. I understand that many people would not approve of this lifestyle. I also understand that this lifestyle has made me successful, confident, happy, mature and flexible – in more ways than one! It's also been part of the reason I've finally learned to be content.

Forced bi. Can we even talk about this? My husband is beyond conservative and very analytical. I love him dearly. My lover is very masculine, outgoing and kinky. Both men are very achievement oriented like I am. One thing I've enjoyed immensely is being able to take such manly men and have them learn to appreciate taking orders from me. Both of these men swore they would never, ever touch another man in any way. They both agreed to play with me and another man, but there could be no contact between the two males. That's hilarious. These two men know so much about me. They both like my drive, passion, and pure lust for sex. They should have known when we started getting in deeper and deeper, that eventually all limits would be revisited. That doesn't mean they have to change, just that we will probably change our limits once we're comfortable with each other. Well, that's what happened. And, one of them was communication with each other. I never dreamed my loving husband would ever be messaging my Dom. I changed a lot of my limits for my Dom. Once I trusted him, I was able to explore an abundance of fetishes I was too scared to try before. Feeling safe with him allowed for that. My husband opened up to allow for this triangle to exist. My husband is my husband is my husband. Do my Dom and I ever talk about if we weren't married, of course! It's not like you can love someone and not have some days when you're thinking to yourself, "I would love to have him/her here with me and here's what we would do!" But, we love our spouses and that's where we are! So after a couple of years, while discussing different topics and fetishes, the subject of the men in my life playing with another man came up once or twice. At first my husband was saying he didn't want to, but he knew it turned me on. My Dom first flat out said no. After a couple of years when the subject came back up, he was much more open-minded. We talked through what that would look like, scenes I would like, how far I would ever want it to go, what he's comfortable with, and if that changed the dynamic of our relationship. We discuss everything at length. He wasn't saying flat no anymore, rather being curious. I secretly think he's always been curious about it although he tells me that people have tried to get him to play MMF before and he said, "HELL NO!" to them. My husband on the other hand, had an experience with it once. We were at a swinger's party. This amazingly hot man came up and wanted to play. The three of us went back to the room and I started sucking him on the bed. He got up to get undressed and my husband came to kneel on the bed beside my face so I could suck him. I did. I'm told I'm amazing at it; so just watching it was turning the other guy on. He slips a condom on his cock and slides in me. He's young, tan, sexy and built. He's so tall that his face is about the same level as mine. Next thing I know he's sucking my husband with me! I was shocked! My husband was shocked! But, he went with it. We all had fun that night with only oral between the two men. Now, here I am bringing it up to him to try again hehehe!

My lover wraps his head around it and I'm giddy! He's agreed to suck if I'll teach him. If he's going to do it, he wants to be good. I don't blame him because I'm an overachiever too! I spend the next couple of weeks going over all the tips and tricks I know. A couple of weeks after that, I have my lover in a hotel room with me. My husband says that he will stop by too and thirty minutes later he's there. We kiss hello and then I instruct them through the process to attempt to make them more comfortable. Is that possible? I'm sure it's very awkward for them, but I manage to coax them through well. I watch my husband drop to his knees while my Dom just stands there watching. I kiss my Dom and I can tell he's nervous. Did I mention these men were wearing panties? They were tasked with wearing panties that they each thought I would like. And whoever picked panties I liked the best got to receive first! It's such a fun little competition for them. My Dom won, so my husband is showing off his skills! My lover is hard as a rock! Mmmm I've taught him well! Then, we switch and it's my lover's turn. He has the biggest, most beautiful lips and I swear they were made for sucking cock! My husband rarely gets hard when someone sucks him other than me. I watch these poor women try for like an hour and I know their jaws have to be sore! I can't help that I'm that good! So, I'm a little apprehensive knowing that my husband may never get hard the very first time my Dom tries being a sissy panty-wearing slut for me. The only way this will work is if he does get hard, so I'm praying my tips and tricks work! I watch my Dom nervously begin to take my husband in his mouth. I can't believe what I'm seeing! He is doing what he swore he wouldn't. He's submitting completely to his Domme. I know he's flipping out. His current bull status is being threatened. But, he's showing me how he's mine. He's exploring something he wouldn't have otherwise. That's awesome. We all end up playing together in a crazy, kinky, sexy threesome with me helping them both suck the other.

The next time we play, my husband and sub are a little more open. I had been telling them how I wanted to see them kiss the next time we all play and so they knew to expect it. When my husband arrived, I had my submissive answer the door. As soon as he entered the room, they kissed! This was the very last thing that they held out on doing, but they did it! Mmmm…my men! They do oral and then my husband fucks my submissive's manpussy! Seriously?! He fills him full and it's so intoxicating to watch the series of events unfold. I don't know how I got this lucky or what I did to deserve these men, but I'm beyond thankful. When they're done, my husband is getting ready to go back to work. My lover and I cuddle on the bed. He tells me bye and leaves with the sight of me snuggled as tight as possible in my Dom's arms. After he leaves, my lover fucks me until I cum.

Another time my lover and I played, we enjoyed each other to the fullest! I was so pleased, excited and satisfied. This time before he left he took the time to say, "The way I see it, there are only two ways this will end. One, she will find out. Two, we will both get tired of this." I'm staring deep into the eyes of my lover, my Dom, my sub... I weigh the options I have for my response. Are you tired of me? Are you tired of this? Are you wanting to leave? No, I said WE get tired of this. Tired of waiting so long to see each other. Tired of being frustrated by not being able to do all the things we want to do, when we want to do them or getting bored of each other. It's a lot to take. I know it's harder for you because you have the freedom I don't have. He knows. He gives you the freedom to play. You have a little more time or can rearrange your schedule easier than I can. I understand. I know. I know it's not fair to you. That doesn't mean that it doesn't matter. It doesn't mean that I don't give a shit. It means that I do everything I can." I look at this man sitting on the bed beside me looking down into my eyes, my soul. He knows me inside and out: physically, emotionally, and mentally. He explains how he understands when I'm so frustrated and can read between the lines of the messages I send. He knows when I do this or that and what those things really mean. My God. This man. He never ceases to amaze me. He may know me better than myself. Is he perfect? Hell no! But, I wouldn't expect him to be or want that.

So option two was fully discussed. He's not bored, nor is he ever going to be. There's no chance in hell I'm going to tire of him. Even the sweet, lovely, intimately things I avoided like the plague with everyone, I crave with him. Option one I didn't push as much. We talked about how his wife's family warned him what would happen if they found out he cheated on her. I asked for specifics and he didn't want to discuss it. He definitely had fear within his eyes and completely bought into what they sold him. They may be prominent, successful and appear to be a kind family, but they have the ability to take out someone that gets out of line. The first time I heard anything about that, I was very uncomfortable. When someone finds out their spouse is cheating, they go into an emotional tailspin. If their family gets involved, especially a woman's Dad or other males in her family, the first thing that happens is that their protective side kicks in. Are they going to kill him? He's completely convinced. Do I need to be concerned for my safety? He doesn't think so because it will all be directed at him. But, I know me. I know that if mine was cheating, I sure as fuck would find out who the bitch is he cheated on me with. I would blame him. My anger would be focused on him, not her. But, I also tend to think very clearly in traumatic situations. Most people don't. I have jokingly warned a staff member during a meeting once to say he/she has never heard of me if someone he/she doesn't know comes in specifically asking for me. There were questions still nagging in the back of my mind about option one. He wouldn't answer specifically what threats had been made to him in the past. I'm not one to let things go. And while that's their marriage, he's still partially mine hehe. And, when shit hits the fan, they may be coming after me too. I'd like to have an idea of what I'm up against. A few days later I ask, "While we're clarifying some things, you said the other day that one way this would be over is if she finds out. Does that mean if she finds out you're going to leave?" In true form of my sexy Dom, his response was "overthinking today huh?" Redirection. Avoiding the part where I actually want an answer. I say 'no, I've had the question for a few days, but I just now asked." His response was "I'd be dead." I froze. My eyes locked on that last word. She loved him. I know she did or she wouldn't fight with him on the occasions she gets an inkling he might be cheating. There's no way that she would let them kill the father of their child. Would she? My mind is swirling around that word. I couldn't imagine my life without him in it. I want more of him. There's no way I could handle him not being here, especially because of an angry parent. Life happens. You may be angry, but you either work through it or move on. You don't end the person! I say, "no you wouldn't be and that wasn't an answer." He says, "that is my answer."

This man risks his marriage and now his life to see me! He risks his life to chat with me and to fuck me. He told me the other day how he wants to make sure his bases are covered 25 times over. Now, I see why. Here I am acting like a petulant brat because I don't get enough time with my Daddy and he's literally risking his life to communicate with me and see me when he can. Talk about feeling two inches tall.

CHAPTER 18

If I were to leave you with parting words of wisdom, I would hope you would remember them. First, don't judge anyone. You're not God. You have no idea what they've been through or why something interests them so much. Ask them. Talk to them. Actively learn about new things and don't snarl your nose at someone if what they do isn't your particular cup of tea. It's okay, everyone's different and you don't have to agree. If you did everyone would be just alike and that would be boring. Second, invest time in yourself. No one has time and it's difficult to make time for anything. But, even if it's just a few minutes a day during your lunchtime, take the time to find out what excites you. What gives you energy? What turns you on? What fuels the fire within you? What do you enjoy? What do you dislike? What is a turn off or bores you? Third, be careful. Don't go into something thinking everyone will understand and you can tell everyone everything. You can't. I wish the world was like that, but the simple truth is that people cannot fully accept other people. For me, I have to be challenged, supported emotionally and sex is a major factor in my lifestyle for happiness. What do you need? Fourth, and most importantly, prioritize everything in your life. Ultimately, here's what matters to me: my faith, my immediate family, my lover, and my job. That's it. Everything else is good too, but everything else falls behind these things. Having a few key priorities in life helps keep you focused on a successful path and protects your happiness.

Know that if you're like me, you're not alone. I'm sure I'm not the only woman juggling the things you've just read. I have so many stories of intense sexual escapades that I could fill a library based on each person. There are others like you. You can be liberated to enjoy your body, enjoy your desires, and enjoy the life you're living. If you keep your priorities in check, you actually can have it all!

While I'm writing this, I receive a message from a sexy black man. He's successful, intelligent and muscular. I'm excited and I can't wait to meet him. My husband and I are planning a vacation out of town with the entire purpose of playing with other people. The man that messaged me lives in the city we will be visiting. I have received hundreds of emails within a day from men that are interested in fucking. This vacation is still two weeks away, so I'll have plenty of yummy men to entertain me! I start adding people to my messaging system. I need to chat with these guys before we get there to know what turns them on, ensure they won't do something that's off limits, and send them sexy pictures to make them rock hard for me before I even get there!

The day of our trip has arrived and I wake up ready to play! We will be traveling in our SUV for hours. My husband has been driving while I was singing my heart out to every song that played on the radio. I was in a maxi dress, no bra, and no panties. My feet were on the dash and my legs are spread wide. He placed his hand between my legs and started to rub. It feels so good. He's obviously a distracted driver. I get a playful gleam in my eye while I tell him to unzip his jeans. I crank the radio up and lean over the seat to suck him. He absolutely loves being sucked while he's driving. I have my knees in my seat. He pulls my dress up over my hips so he can finger me while I'm sucking him. Everyone that drives past us can see my naked juicy pussy on full display. I hear a loud truck approach and he won't let me stop. We find a place to pull over and it happens to be near a graveyard. He bends me over a confederate soldier's tombstone. I am trying to tell him how wrong it is and how we'll get caught, but apparently a graveyard is a fantasy of his. I apologize to soldiers and their families.

I arrange to meet these men at a local swingers club and after we check into our hotel, I change into the outfit my husband selected for me to wear. I have 20 men that may be meeting me over the two evenings I'm in town, so I want to make sure I look hot as fuck for them. I put on my ultra high heels and over up with my fur coat. I look like a high priced hooker and that's exactly how I had hoped he would have me dressed! My phone is full of pictures of cocks, handsome faces, sexy women showing off their big boobs and couples that are engaged in crazy fun sex acts! I can't wait for this weekend of fun to get started!

I get in the car and we make our way to the club. We check in and go to find a seat. We need somewhere to place our things while we go look around. He takes my coat and deposits it into a chair, then leads me down a hallway toward a playroom. My husband and I like to get a feel for a facility before we do anything. I notice a skinny, hot blonde woman checking him out. I smile at her and he has no idea that she wants him. I'll have to remember to persuade her to flirt with him and fuck him later. I round the corner to see an enormous open playroom with wall-to-wall mattresses. That's so fun! I can't wait to put on a show in this room! While I'm dreaming up different acts I want to show off, I feel a hand grab my ass and a man is pressing his hard dick into my back. Before I can turn around, he says, "Hello Scarlett. I've been waiting for you to arrive" in a deep masculine voice. My pulse quickens as I feel his hand slide up between my thighs. I have no panties on, so his fingers feel the moist opening immediately. He moans in my ear and I gasp as he shoves his fingers inside. The identity of the mysterious, groping stranger is driving me wild. I need to know who is about to ravage me.

www.ingramcontent.com/pod-product-compliance
Lightning Source LLC
LaVergne TN
LVHW011224080426
835509LV00005B/308